George Everston Woodward, Francis W. Woodward

Woodward's architecture, Landscape Gardening and Rural Art

Volume 1

George Everston Woodward, Francis W. Woodward

Woodward's architecture, Landscape Gardening and Rural Art
Volume 1

ISBN/EAN: 9783337080501

Printed in Europe, USA, Canada, Australia, Japan

Cover: Foto ©Andreas Hilbeck / pixelio.de

More available books at **www.hansebooks.com**

WOODWARD'S ARCHITECTURE,

LANDSCAPE GARDENING, AND RURAL ART.

No. I.—1867.

BY

GEO. E. & F. W. WOODWARD,

EDITORS OF THE "HORTICULTURIST;" AUTHORS OF "WOODWARD'S COUNTRY HOMES," "WOODWARD'S GRAPERIES," ETC.

NEW YORK:
GEO. E. & F. W. WOODWARD, 37 PARK ROW,
OFFICE OF THE "HORTICULTURIST."
1867.

Entered, according to Act of Congress, in the Year 1866, by

GEO. E. & F. W. WOODWARD,

in the Clerk's Office of the District Court for the Southern District of New York.

Davies & Kent,
Electrotypers and Stereotypers,
183 William St., N. Y.

PREFACE.

This is the first number of a permanent Annual Publication, to be issued from the Office of the "Horticulturist," and intended to supply a demand for plans and information in all departments of Rural Art. Each number will be thoroughly illustrated with original and practical designs, adapted to the requirements of men of moderate means.

CONTENTS.

Design No. 1.
Design for an Ice-House.................................... 11

Design No. 2.
Cottage, with Plans 13

Design No. 3.
A Compact Cottage, with Plans............................. 15

Design No. 4.
An Octagonal Cottage, with Plans 17

Design No. 5.
A Farm Cottage.. 19

Designs Nos. 6 and 7.
Ice-Houses, with Plans.................................... 21

Designs Nos. 8 and 9.
Ornaments in Landscape Gardening.......................... 23
Well-House 25

Design No. 10.
Cottage and Plans 27

Design No. 11.
Cottage and Plans... 29

Design No. 12.
Drying-House for Fruits................................... 30

Design No. 13.
Plan for Laying Out a Square Acre Lot 31
Ornamental Roads.. 32

Design No. 14.
A Farm House.. 39

Design No. 15.
A Southern House 40

CONTENTS.

Design No. 16.
A Cottage Stable	42
A Bird-House	45

Design No. 17.
Plan for Laying Out a Three-Acre Lot	46
Chicken-Coops	47

Design No. 18.
A Small Stable ... 49

Design No. 19.
Plan for Improving Lot of Four Acres	51
" " " " Five "	51

Design No. 20.
Cottage, with Plans ... 53

Design No. 21.
Porter's Lodge	55
Well-House	56

Design No. 22.
A Barn, with Plans ... 57

Design No. 23.
A Parsonage House ... 59

Design No. 24.
Cottage, with Tower ... 61

Design No. 25.
Cottage and Plans ... 63

Design No. 26.
Cottage and Plans ... 65

Design No. 27.
Cottage and Plans ... 67

Designs Nos. 28 and 29.
Canopied Seat	68
A Rustic Seat	68

Design No. 30.
Small Cottage, with Designs and Plans for Future Additions	69
Design for a Fountain	73

CONTENTS. vii

Design No. 31.
	PAGE
A Suburban Cottage	75
Hitching Post and Steps	77

Design No. 32.
Plan for Laying Out a Lot One Hundred by Two Hundred Feet... 78

Design No. 33.
Tool-House, etc., with Plan... 79

Design No. 34.
A Piggery and Plan... 80

Design No. 35.
Smoke-Houses... 81

Design No. 36.
Plan for Laying Out Five Acres... 82

Design No. 37.
Plan for Laying Out a Lot Seventy-five by One Hundred and Fifty Feet.. 83

Design No. 38.
A Square Cottage... 85

Design No. 39.
A Doctor's Residence.. 87
Design for a Well-House... 89

Design No. 40.
Ice-House, Cooling-Room, Tool-House, and Workshop combined.. 90

Designs Nos. 41 and 42.
Plan for Laying Out a Lot Fifty by One Hundred and Fifty Feet   91
"   "   "   an Irregular Plot..................................... 91

Design No. 43.
Cottage and Plans.. 93

Design No. 44.
A Chicken-House.. 94

Design No. 45.
Plan for Laying Out a Lot One Hundred and Fifty by Two Hundred Feet.. 95

CONTENTS.

Design No. 46.
A Barn, with Plan.................................... 96

Design No. 47.
Plan for Laying Out a Plot of about Two Acres............ 97

Design No. 48.
How to Remodel an Old House......................... 98
The Old House Remodeled............................ 100

Design No. 49.
Plan for Laying Out a Lot of One Acre................. 102

Design No. 50.
Plan for Laying Out a Lot of Two Acres................ 103
Computing Cost of Building........................... 104
Design for Gateway.................................. 105

Design No. 51.
Timber Cottage...................................... 106

Design No. 52.
Plan for Laying Out a Lot Two Hundred and Fifty by Three Hundred and Twenty-five Feet........................ 109

Design No. 53.
Design for a Barn................................... 110

Design No. 54.
A Farm Cottage..................................... 111

Design No. 55.
A Farm House....................................... 113

Design No. 56.
Plan for Laying Out a Ten-Acre Lot.................... 115

Design No. 57.
A Country School-House.............................. 117
Design for Entrance Gate............................ 119

Design No. 58.
Design for Grape Arbor.............................. 120

THOSE who have watched the progress of Rural Architecture for some years past, have noticed a marked advance in architectural design and proportion and convenient and economical interior arrangement; yet, compared with the large number of structures yearly put up, the really attractive and tasteful buildings form the exception, and not the rule. Building, at best, is an expensive undertaking, and those who engage in it without availing themselves of the progressive improvements of the day, make investments from which it is difficult to realize first cost; while he who embraces the principles of beauty, harmony, good taste, etc., rarely fails to command his customer, and a handsome profit when ready to sell. The fact we desire to impress most thoroughly is, that it costs no more to build correctly and beautifully than to ignore all rules of taste, and that every one in this broad land who means to have a home of his own, should have a home worth owning.

The designs shown are mostly of a low-priced description, and the prevailing style chosen is the rural Gothic, the best that is known for cottage structures, being the most economical and useful. Nearly all the designs admit of shingle roofs, which places the workmanship under the owner's control. In new countries, slate and tin roofers, and their materials, are not always available. Handy farm-laborers can shave shingles and make their own roofs; and the pioneer, the well-to-do farmer, the laborer, and the mechanic usually expect to aid in erecting their own buildings.

It is proposed, however, to introduce all the varied styles of architecture in future numbers, and they may be looked for with interest as supplying from year to year the latest and best models in the progress of Rural Art.

A moderate number of plans for laying out small tracts of land are given; and as our descriptions must necessarily be brief, the illustrations have been so managed as to tell their own story. Many designs for necessary out-buildings are introduced, as the plan of this book covers all departments of Rural Art. No pains or expense have been spared in making this work reliable. All designs are of a practical character, can be enlarged and worked from; many of them are from actual construction, and all are worth study and attention from any one who contemplates building. We mean that it shall supply a want long felt for designs for convenient and attractive homes for the million. We are largely indebted for assistance in preparing the designs to Mr. E. C. Hussey. Most of the engravings are by Mr. Chas. Spiegle, both of whom have executed their work in a thoroughly artistic and satisfactory manner

Fig. 2.—Design for an Ice-House.

Fig. 3.—Cottage.

   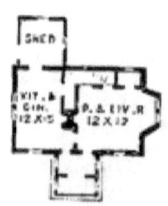   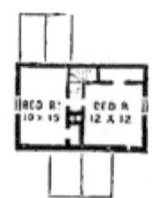

Fig. 4.—Cellar Plan.   Fig. 5.—First Floor.   Fig. 6.—Second Floor.

DESIGN No. 2.

A LOW-PRICED COTTAGE.

This design of two rooms on each floor gives a good deal of available space with independent entrances to each room. To those who must have houses at the lowest possible sum, the bay-window, porch, and finials may be omitted at first, and added at a future day; but by all means preserve the broad projecting roof and the general outline as shown. Let the first-floor ceiling be 8 feet, and use studding of the usual length of 13 feet; this will give a breast of about 3½ feet in second story. Make the height in center 8 feet, and the roof about one third to one half pitch; that is, the height of the roof should be one third or one half the width of the building. Additions can be made at any time when wanted, and will rather add to than detract from the general appearance. The cost of this cottage will range all the way from $600 to $1,200; and this difference exists in nearly all classes of buildings, according to the section of country in which they are built, the facility of getting materials, and the business management of the owner. As prices are constantly changing, it is useless to make statements that are only calculated to mislead; indeed, at no former period could prices be furnished without creating much mischief. The best way is to show the nearest good mechanic the design, tell him, as near as possible, your wishes, and he can give the most reliable figures.

Fig. 7.—A Compact Cottage.

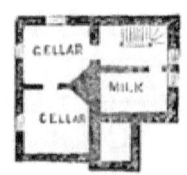

Fig. 8.—Cellar Plan.

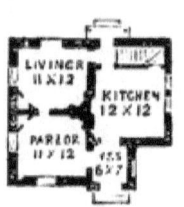

Fig. 9.—First Floor.

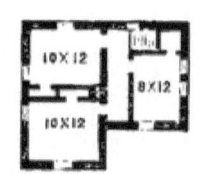

Fig. 10.—Second Floor.

DESIGN No. 3.

A COMPACT COTTAGE.

We show here a design for a very pretty, compact cottage, that may be erected either with wood, stone, or brick. Rock-faced rubble masonry, over which vines may be trained, would, we think, be very suitable. Those who build houses like this can easily find purchasers for them; indeed, acre-lots in the suburbs of our cities and larger villages, with tasty cottages and a moderate amount of landscape embellishment, would not remain uncalled-for many days. There is a certain steady demand for cosy, comfortable homes adapted to the purses of the great masses that should attract more attention from capitalists. Any convenient locality, where the nucleus, composed of a store, a church, a school-house, and a first-rate hotel, can be established, could be made very attractive, and induce many to leave the crowded and unhealthy tenements of the city for a home in the country, be it ever so small. The complete cost of such an establishment in the country, at a less distance in point of time from the City Hall of New York city than Thirty-fifth Street, would not exceed the yearly rental of a not much more commodious house in the city, while its annual increasing value amounts to more than the legal rate of interest.

Fig. 11.—An Octagonal Cottage.

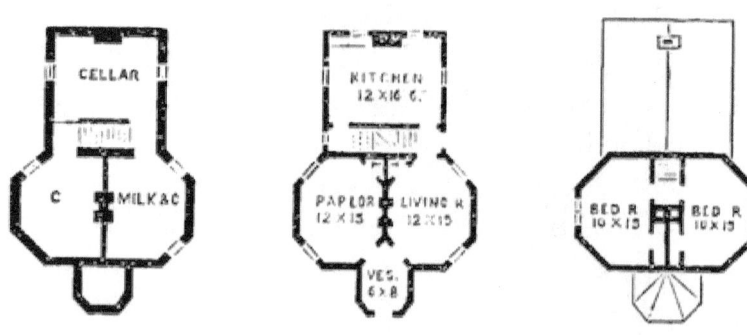

Fig. 12.—Cellar Plan. Fig. 13.—First Floor. Fig. 14.—Second Floor.

DESIGN No. 4.

AN OCTAGONAL COTTAGE.

For the sake of a little variety in form, we here introduce a cottage having octagonal ends, and the principal rooms on the first floor of octagonal form. These rooms, furnished with a fair degree of taste, will present a cosy appearance. The roof covers the building in the same manner as if it had square corners, and is supported by a neat bracket of timber-work. Those who do not fancy this suggestion, can adopt a similar plan with square angles at the corners, and omit the brackets under the roof. The arrangement of the windows in the octagon ends gives better facilities for ventilation than if both windows were on the same line of wall, which they would have to be to preserve the symmetry of a square room. In the construction of this house use the "balloon frame," because it is stronger and forty per cent. cheaper than any other—for a full illustrated description of which see "Woodward's Country Homes." Instead of filling in with brick, sheath the outside of the studding horizontally with rough boards, and over this put the siding; a layer of tarred paper placed between would be serviceable. This will make a strong, warm house.

Fig. 15.—A Farm-Cottage.

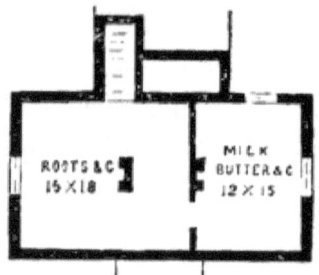

Fig. 16.—Cellar Plan.

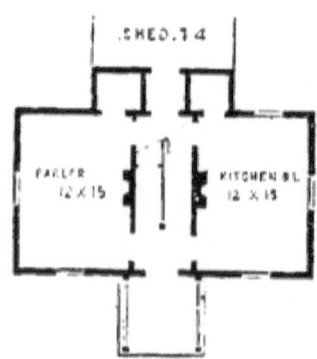

Fig. 17.—First Floor.

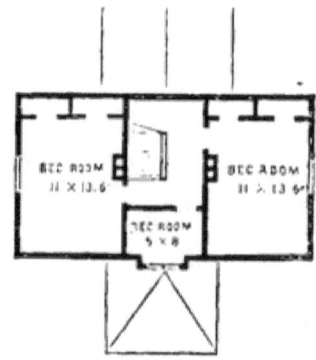

Fig. 18.—Second Floor.

DESIGN No. 5.

A FARM COTTAGE.

This design will answer well for a farm-cottage, presents a good variety, and would be considered an attractive home. We have had in view a moderate expenditure, and of course the builder must be satisfied with a moderate amount of room. Prices we might give, if we were satisfied they would be any guide; but a book like this, having a national circulation, can not be of any value whatever as to cost of construction. We have seen the time when, in the immediate vicinity of New York, this cottage could be built for $500, or even less. It might possibly be built now for $1,200; yet in some sections of the country, labor and materials can be had for half the prices they command here. There are many portions of the West where, at the present time (fall of 1866), this cottage could be fully completed for $400 to $500. An ingenious farmer, who can supply from his farm a considerable portion of the materials, do his own hauling, and with the aid of a skillful mechanic and one or two handy laborers, if the work be not pushed on too fast, could execute this and similar designs by the use of very little money.

Fig. 19.—Ice-House.

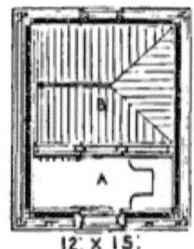

12 x 15.
Fig. 20.—Plan of Fig. 19.

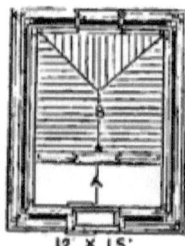

12 x 15.
Fig. 21.—Plan of Fig. 22.

Fig. 22.—Ice-House.

DESIGNS Nos. 6 AND 7.

ICE-HOUSES.

Ice is an article that may, with many, be considered indispensable. Those who have enjoyed its use are unwilling to do without it. The comforts of the household are materially increased, and an abundant supply is a great luxury.

Ice-houses may be constructed to suit all tastes and purses; and the various designs we give can be built plainly as well as elaborately. About twelve feet cube of ice is the requisite quantity for most families, and a bulk of this size keeps better than if smaller. The best houses are those built entirely above ground, though one, as shown in fig. 19, which is built into a gravelly bank is not objectionable. Thorough drainage is essential, and where a pipe is used, it should be trapped, to prevent a current of air. The sides should be double, with from 8 to 12 inches space, and packed with wet tan, sawdust, or pulverized charcoal, well rammed down. Sometimes double walls of this kind are made, with an air chamber between; and sometimes an air chamber is made by furring out and lining with boards only. At the bottom we prefer, after the drainage has been provided, to lay a good plank floor; cover this with 6 or 8 inches of sawdust or tan, and then pack the ice (which should be from 6 to 8 inches or more in thickness) in layers, putting the blocks as close together as possible, and chinking up with small pieces of ice or snow. A space of about 6 inches should be left between the mass of ice and the sides of the house, which should be thoroughly packed with sawdust or tan. When the house is full, put over all the ice a layer of sawdust or tan at least one foot in thickness, and pack it down thoroughly. A good roof should be provided, and ventilation of a most thorough character. A draft of air through the ice would soon destroy it; a draft of air above it only is an essential preservative. In constructing these houses, it would be better, in addition to the openings shown, to leave a space from six inches to one foot wide, under the eaves, above the plate, both sides the entire length of the house. This opening is protected from the rain, and the free admission of air thus secured is of great advantage.

Straw and hay are used sometimes for packing in place of sawdust or tan, but are not so serviceable. In each of these designs there is a cooling-room attached for milk, butter, meats, fruits, etc., marked A on the plans. The room marked B is the one in which the ice is packed; the floor is laid so that the drainage runs to one point, and is carried off by a pipe trapped, to prevent the admission of air.

ORNAMENTS IN LANDSCAPE GARDENING.

DESIGN No. 8.

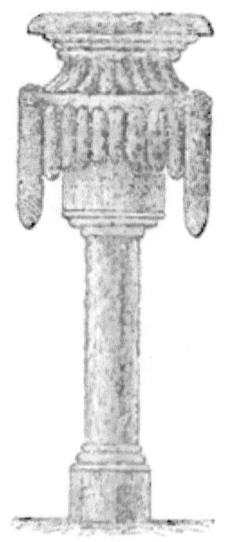

Fig. 23.—Rustic Stand.

Wild ground and irregular surfaces call for rude and bold work. Here introduce rustic bridges crossing ravines, rustic seats, vases, baskets of rustic work, gnarled and curious roots encircling boxes of plants, hollow stumps and dead trees supporting climbing plants, rustic kiosks on spots which offer agreeable resting-places and command fine views; all such objects are appropriate to grounds so characterized. There is no particular beauty in a piece of rustic work in itself, but when properly placed it becomes beautiful from its association, and in turn enhances the picturesque of the grounds about.

DESIGN No. 9.

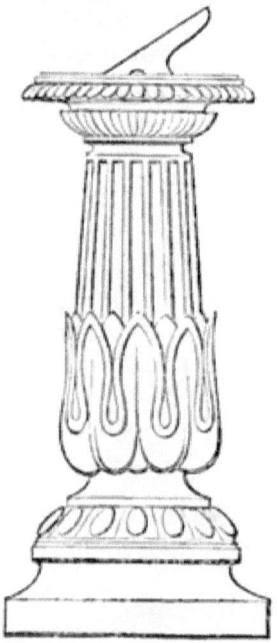

Fig. 24.—Sun-Dial.

Among the many objects used for adornment, there is a very pretty one which we would like to see more frequently employed, and which when properly placed by the side of some walk well retired from other objects, is in itself highly suggestive. We refer to the *Sun-dial*. What thoughts this monitor suggests to the mind! how silent, yet how eloquent! His must be a vacant mind indeed who can pass such a teacher without finding thought to accompany his walk. A shadow teacheth us, and we learn in the end that we have pursued but shadows.

In the beautiful words of the poet:

> "This shadow on the dial's face,
>   That steals from day to day,
> With slow, unseen, unceasing pace,
>   Moments, and months, and years away;
> This shadow, which in every clime,
>   Since light and motion first began,
> Hath held its course sublime—
>   What is it? Mortal man!
> It is the scythe of time—
>   A shadow only to the eye;
> Yet in its calm career
>   It levels all beneath the sky;
> And still, through each succeeding year
> Right onward with resistless power,
> Its stroke shall darken every hour,
> Till nature's race be run,
> And time's last shadow shall eclipse the sun."

Fig. 25.—Well-House.

Fig. 26.—Perspective.

Fig. 27.—Cellar Plan.

Fig. 28.—First Floor.

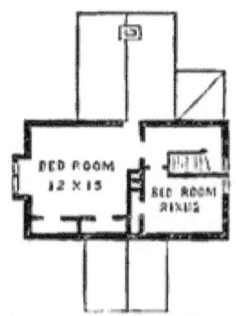

Fig. 29.—Second Floor.

DESIGN No. 10.

The additions of porches, verandas, bay-windows, etc., increase the effect of cottage-houses to a very considerable degree, add much to interior convenience and beauty, and, if put on at the time when the building is constructed, do not materially augment the expense. We think they are always worth their full cost, and rarely fail to make an impression upon the eye of a purchaser. The interior wood-work of this cottage, or any other, should be selected with some little care, and all stained —either satin-wood or light black-walnut. These stains, which can be easily procured, are better if laid on in oil, and then, if covered with two coats of varnish, make the nearest approach possible to the appearance of the above-named natural woods. No grainer's art can do as well. Handsomely stained and varnished wood-work is, we think, the most superior mode of treating interiors. It adds much to the warmth and cosiness of the rooms, has the effect of furnishing, and, so far as cleanliness is concerned, is of great help to the housekeeper. This style of finish, whether for the humble cottage or costly mansion, is better and more attractive, if done with good taste, than the most costly and elaborately painted tints.

Fig. 30.

Fig. 31.—Cellar Plan.

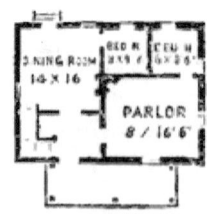

Fig. 32.—First Floor.

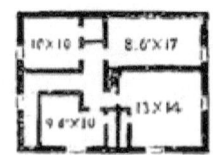

Fig. 33.—Second Floor.

DESIGN No. 11.

This design can, for the amount of room afforded, be constructed very cheaply. The kitchen is shown in the basement plan, but can be put on the first floor, or in a rear addition, if deemed more convenient. If built in an exposed situation, some filling-in between the studding will be necessary. There are several modes of doing this, all of which add to the stiffness and solidity of the frame, and ward off the searching winds. An air chamber for confined or dead air adds much to winter warmth and summer coolness, and this is usually provided for. The most common mode of filling-in is with soft brick laid on edge in mortar; grout is also made use of. Back plastering, or lathing between studs—nailing common laths or rough pieces against strips fastened to each side of the studs and covered with coarse mortar—is serviceable. Where lumber is plenty, cover the frame with rough boards, and put the weather-boarding on the outside of the rough boarding; this we have found answers an excellent purpose. A layer of common tarred roofing-paper between the two courses of boarding will render the house impenetrable to wind or rain, and affords one of the best means of protection.

DESIGN No. 12.

A HOUSE FOR DRYING FRUITS.

The following sketch, received from J. C. Hobson, Esq., Cardington, Ohio, is of a building of moderate dimensions, 4 by 12 feet, and 5 feet in height, set upon a wall of brick or stone 20 inches high; and to obviate the necessity of going inside when heated up for drying, it is constructed with two tiers of drawers on either side, 23 inches by 5 feet, with slat or wire bottoms, each one made to slide in and out independent of the rest, and each tier inclosed with double doors. The building is heated by means of furnaces extending from either end, and communicating with the flue in the center.

FIG. 34.—DRYING-HOUSE.

By reason of the drawers meeting over the furnaces in the middle, the heat in rising is compelled to pass through them, thus the fruit is dried faster than by the usual mode of placing it on shelves against the wall of the house.

The number of drawers may be increased to double the amount represented in the drawing, if necessary, which would make them hold a considerable quantity of fruit, say from twenty to thirty bushels.

DESIGN No. 13.

PLAN FOR LAYING OUT A SQUARE ACRE LOT.

BY E. FERRAND, DETROIT, MICH.

Fig. 35.

A, Dwelling.
B, Piazza.
C, Passage from the Barn to the Street.
D, Greenhouse.
E, Grapery (house).
F, Flower-beds.
H, Kitchen Garden, with dwarf fruit-trees and small fruits.
K, Trellis of grapevines.
L, Yard.
M, Gate.
N, Gate.
O, Stable, Barn, and other Out-buildings.

ORNAMENTAL ROADS.

A PROPER location of an ornamental road adds to it, we may say, all of its character and importance, and it may be made in inexperienced hands a very tame and meaningless affair. To locate and make a road that shall fulfill only a useful purpose is one thing; to so locate it that it shall comply with all the requisites sought for in ornamental grounds, is quite another matter. Whatever there is of consequence should be made the most of, and by the most graceful and easy lines of curvature should destroy the thought that anything of the kind was intended. The entrance, the perspective view of the dwelling, the easy grade, the drainage, construction, planting, etc., are only thoroughly considered by those of extensive practice.

Where proper materials for road metal can not be had, or where expense is to be avoided, the earth road must be adopted. To make this is an easy matter; thorough drainage, wherever necessary, should be most carefully done. The bed of the road should have a crowning of about 4 inches in a width of 16 feet, or half an inch to a foot, both ways from sides, as shown in fig. 36. The sods at the edge should be kept low—not over 1½ inches high, except in such cases as where surface drainage crosses the road, and is liable to wash earth on to the lawn. The grade line in the direction of the road should be kept as regular as possible, and avoid undulating. On the surface of the

AND RURAL ART. 33

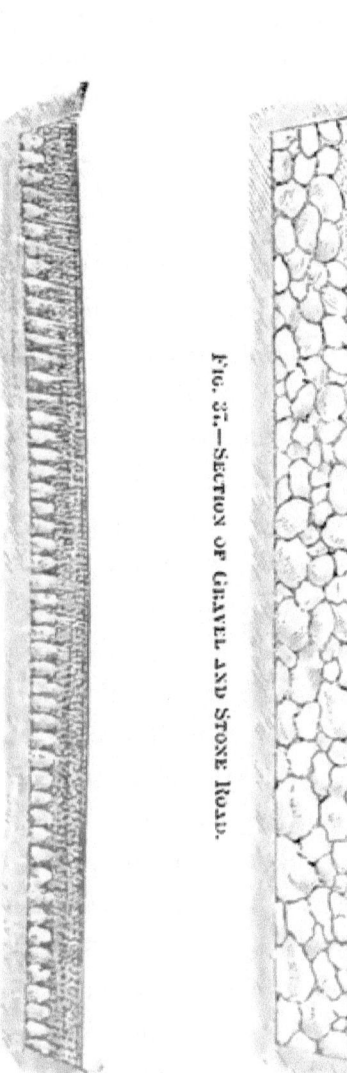

Fig. 2.—Section of Telford Road.

Fig. 35.—Section of Gravel and Stone Road.

Fig. 36.—Section of Earth Road.

road, gravel, coal ashes, oyster shells, or similar materials, may be placed to good advantage, and will make good roads through all the dry seasons. The making of an earth road similar to this is in all cases necessary where the road bed is to be stoned, except that it is taken out to a greater depth. The most common mode of making a stone road is after the manner shown in fig. 37. Stones of unequal size are laid in, or usually thrown in, to a depth varying according to the builder's notion, generally one foot and over, and covered with 4 to 6 inches of gravel. The chief objection to it is, that it requires a larger amount of excavation; if the stones are not carefully hand-packed and rolled, they are liable to work out on the surface; heavy loads, as coal, hay, manure, etc., will cut them up, and weeds will grow thickly and rapidly. In a park, on properly constructed roads in constant use by light carriages, these objections would have no weight. Still, by a greater expenditure of labor in keeping them in order, such roads, when well made, answer a very good purpose; but as an investment they are not so good as other kinds that do not require so much care. The first cost is less than broken stone roads. They should not, under ordinary circumstances, exceed 10 inches of thickness of stone and gravel.

Fig. 38 illustrates the manner of constructing the Telford road, a valuable and well-tested plan, good in all localities where stone can be had, and admits of a softer and inferior quality of stone being used in the pavement. Telford approved of a level cross grade instead of a convex surface. Hughes, a later author, declares the convex

AND RURAL ART.

Fig. 39.—Section of McAdam Road.

Fig. 40.—Section of Baildon Road.

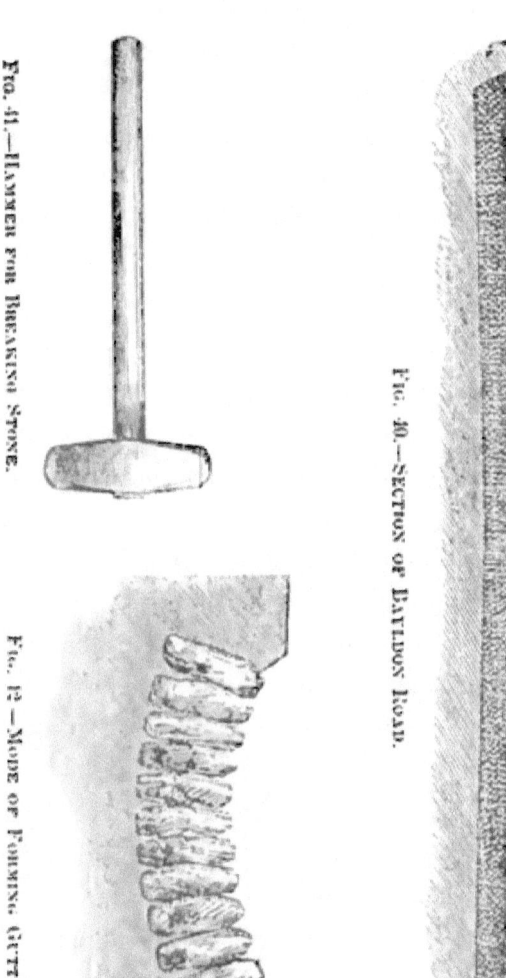

Fig. 41.—Hammer for Breaking Stone.

Fig. 42.—Mode of Forming Gutters.

line to be the best, which it undoubtedly is. This road is made by first setting a rough pavement of stone, as shown in fig. 37. The projections of the upper part are broken off with a hammer, and the interstices are packed with stone chips or spawls. On this pavement are placed two layers of road metal, and the whole is covered with gravel or some other good binding material. The whole thickness for an ornamental road need not be over 10 to 12 inches.

Fig. 39 shows the manner of making the McAdam road. This consists entirely of road metal; that is, stone broken to a cubical form of $2\frac{1}{2}$ inches, and put on in three layers, each of which is worked together by carriage wheels, and the final surface made smooth by constant use. It becomes in time a solid, compact, impenetrable body, the stone uniting by its own angles, aided by the dust ground from them by constant use. This class of road-making is not adapted for private estates, in consequence of the time and use required to make the surface smooth; and the fine dust is objectionable.

Fig. 40 is a cross section of what is known as the Bayldon system, and is, we think, the most superior manner known of constructing either public highways or private ornamental roads. It consists of a layer of road metal 6 inches in thickness placed on in one solid body, thoroughly rolled, and covered with about $1\frac{1}{2}$ inches of blending material, good gravel being the best. We have, however, in an extensive practice, built these roads with a layer of road metal of 4 to 5 inches thick, and with just gravel enough to finish the surface even, one of which, after eight years of constant use, does not appear to have failed in the slightest particular. It has, through all seasons, presented a hard, smooth, handsome surface. This system of road-making requires the least quantity of excavation, and can be made ready for use at once. Its construction is the simplest of all modes, and its durability and efficiency have stood the test of thirty years.

The prevailing impression is, that the stone and gravel road, fig. 37, is the cheapest to construct; a very doubtful matter, we think, compared with the Bayldon plan. One thing is certain, however, that to keep the stone and gravel road in polished order, in private estates, requires at least four times the care; and if a little is saved in first cost, it is soon balanced by additional expense. Where economy in building a good road is to be considered, the stone might be broken at leisure intervals through the winter, and by those unfitted by age or misfortune from doing the work of able-bodied men. The stone is broken with a steel hammer weighing about $1\frac{3}{4}$ lbs. (see fig. 41). The stone-breaker sits at his work, and soon becomes very expert. Some use long-handled hammers, and stand up, but can not accomplish much.

Where it becomes necessary to form gutters, we think it best to do so with quarried or fractured stone put together in the usual manner of making a pavement (see fig. 42). The advantage is, that the gravel may be raked in a thin layer on the gutter (which is always unsightly), and the ragged edges of the stone will hold it, and prevent its being washed. Cobblestone gutters answer a good purpose, but can not be so easily concealed.

Fig. 43.—A Farm-House

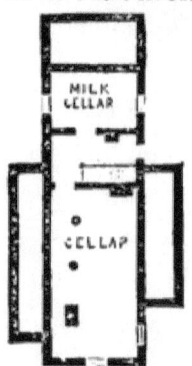

Fig. 44.—Cellar Plan.

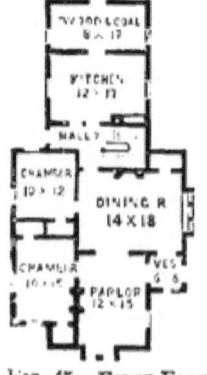

Fig. 45.—First Floor.

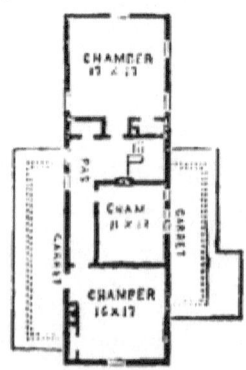

Fig. 46.—Second Floor.

DESIGN No. 14.

A FARM-HOUSE.

This design is for a farm-house of an irregular exterior form, covered by a roof without valleys, except those by the dormer window.

As the plan provides for sleeping-rooms on the first floor, about the healthiness of which opinions differ, we quote the following from the New York *Tribune* reports of the discussions of the New York Farmers' Club:

"*Sleeping-Rooms, are Elevated Ones most Healthy?* —Isaac Bond, Washington City.—'Are low-story rooms equally healthy as lodging rooms with those of upper stories? I have long been led, perhaps more by prejudice, or the opinions of others, than by facts or good reasons, to believe up-stairs decidedly the better; but finding the one-story plans given in Miss Beecher's book, without a hint or misgiving as to their being less healthful, while the sole or chief object of the work, which appears excellent in all other respects, so far as I have read it, is to improve the health of American women, I have been led to question my old opinions, and to inquire whether sleeping on the first floor would do more harm to my whole family of five, than going to the second story about ten times a day would do my wife, who is not very strong, and two very young daughters? If you can furnish facts or sound reasons bearing upon this question, they will

DESIGN No. 15.

A SOUTHERN HOUSE.

Fig. 17. Perspective View.

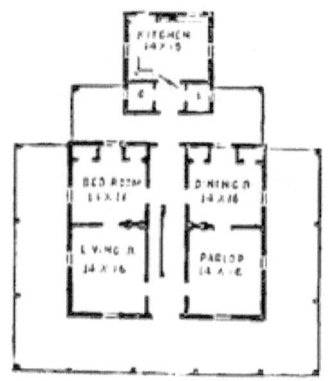

Fig. 18.—First Floor.

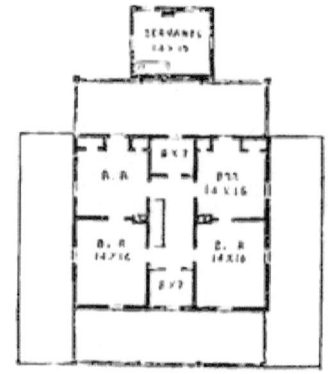

Fig. 19.—Second Floor.

doubtless benefit many others no less than myself. I may add that economy in building is a very important consideration with me, and I am fully aware that a second story is the cheapest way of getting the same amount of additional room to what we must have in the first story, two rooms, besides wood-shed, etc., as you advise in a late number of the *Tribune*. My situation is on one acre, three miles N.N.W. of the Post-office Department.'

"SOLON ROBINSON—Let us look at a few simple facts, which may, perhaps, upset the writer's prejudice about the unhealthiness of lodging in lower rooms. Nearly all of the ancient farm-houses of New England had one, and frequently three or four beds upon the lower floor. The people in those days certainly were no more unhealthy than they were after it became fashionable to build two or three story houses. About the cruelest wrong of all that a man of ample grounds can inflict upon his family is to build a house which compels them often to traverse long flights of stairs. I am well satisfied, from personal experience and observation, that a properly constructed one-story house upon a dry soil is just as healthy for lodgings upon its lower floor as a higher house would be upon its upper ones. Mr. Bond speaks of the economy of space gained in making two-story houses instead of one. Should the health, comfort, and life of the occupants be sacrificed to economy? Besides, it is only economy in the first cost of building material; in all after-years it is a serious loss of labor to all the family who are compelled to ascend to an upper story daily, and frequently hourly, to perform their necessary household duties. An upstairs sick room

DESIGN No. 16.

A COTTAGE STABLE.

Fig. 50.—Perspective View.

Fig. 51.—Plan.

is particularly inconvenient. It is bad enough for people who live in cities to suffer from such disadvantages. It is positively wicked for a man building in the country to ape the fashion of city houses. Be assured, sir, there is no reason why the lower rooms of a one-story country house should be unhealthy for lodging. Probably one of the main reasons why houses have of late years been built so high is owing to the expensiveness of roofing materials. That difficulty is likely now to be obviated. Roofing made cheap, durable, and safe from danger of fire will tend to a great improvement in the style of our farmhouses. If we discuss the subject enough to awaken the public mind to a sense of its importance, we shall one of these days get back to the comforts of one-story houses.

"R. H. WILLIAMS—I entirely agree with the opinions expressed by Mr. Robinson. I would never recommend building a farm-house over one and a half story high. That is the most economical, as that form will afford all the sleeping-rooms necessary to be placed on the upper floor, at a much less cost than they could be made in a full-storied house, and, besides, it looks more fitting as a farm-house. A two or three story house is inconsistent with the wants of the farm, and shows bad judgment in those who build them. This is one of the most important questions we have had before the Club, and one which affords room for ample discussion. It is sometimes very remarkable to see how one man gives fashion and form to all the dwellings in the vicinity. If some pretentious builder leads off with a high-storied house, no matter how inconvenient, others are very apt to ape the fashion. In one section of this State, the almost universal style is a two-story center, with two one-story wings. The most that can be said of that form is, that it is fashionable. Anything that we can say here to improve the style of farm-houses will be beneficial to a great many people.

"Mr. DISTURNELL contested against lower-floor lodging-rooms, because he was satisfied they were much more unhealthy than upper ones. He endeavored to prove it from some statistics drawn from Cairo, Egypt.

"Mr. ROBINSON said his position was taken for a dry, hard, rocky soil, like that of New England generally, and not for malarious Egypt.

"The CHAIRMAN said that Judge Butler, formerly a physician at Norwalk, Conn., declares that when people were in the habit of sleeping in lower rooms, maladies prevailed which are now seldom heard of, such as a low grade of fevers. He says prevailing fogs never rise above fourteen feet high, and those sleeping in upper rooms escape its influence. His recommendation to all who build country houses is to make the cellar under the entire house, cementing the bottom and sides so thoroughly that no gas can arise from the earth; and never to sleep on the lower floor. Besides keeping the cellar clean, care should also be taken to clean the well every year. Dr. Ward, who lives near the great salt-marshes of New Jersey, says, from his house, which is situated on a hill, he can look down upon the banks of fog lying upon a lower level. All of our sleeping-rooms are upon the upper floors, and, I think, in a more healthy stratum of the atmosphere than they would be if less elevated.

"Dr. SNODGRASS—This may be so in that locality, but there are others where the case is reversed. Those living immediately upon the banks of the Potomac, and other Southern rivers, have often escaped malarious diseases, while the houses situated upon the adjoining hills or bluffs were so sickly some seasons as scarcely to be habitable.

"HENRY WARD BEECHER—A few miles south of Indianapolis, upon a high bluff of White River, one of the highest in that locality, in the early settlement of the country, there was a town built. Upon the opposite side of the river there was a small settlement, but slightly elevated, upon the water level. According to the usual theory about malaria, these houses should have been sickly, and those in the town healthy; the reverse was the fact to such a degree that the town was entirely abandoned, and the houses left to decay and waste. The laws of health are not always to be measured by high or low situations, nor by high or low sleeping-rooms, if they are properly ventilated."

FIG. 52.- A BIRD-HOUSE.

DESIGN No. 17.

PLAN FOR LAYING OUT A THREE-ACRE LOT.

BY E. FERRAND, DETROIT, MICH.

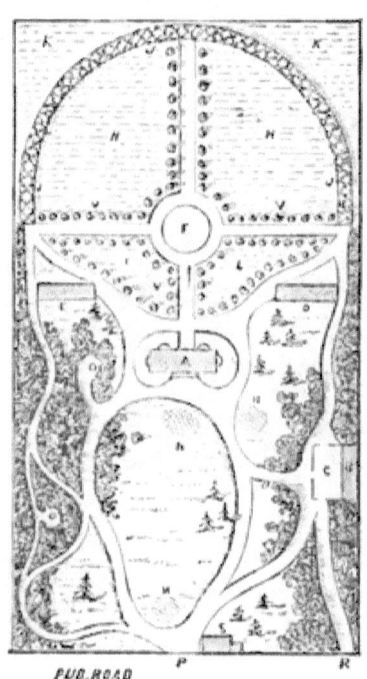

Fig. 53.

A, Dwelling-House.
B, Stable, Barn, etc.
C, Barn-yard, with three openings.
D, Grapery.
E, Greenhouse.
F, Water.
H, Kitchen Garden.
I, Grapevine Arbor.
K, Place for small fruits.
L, Strawberries.
N, Flower-beds.
O, Places for rustic seats.
P, Principal Entrance.
R, Entrance to the Barn.
S, Gardener's House.
V, Dwarf fruit trees.

This garden has the appearance of a much larger place than it really is; in fact, the plan could be applied to a place of ten or more acres just as well as to the limited space of three. The roads are numerous. It is intended for a lot in the proximate vicinity of the city, and to be occupied by a man who has means to keep it in order.

All these gardens are intended for the same purpose, and laid out according to the same principle; that is to say, the most is done to conceal their narrow limits, and leave one to guess how far one may be from the end of it when one is no more than ten feet from the well-concealed fence; at the same time, all the secondary buildings, such as barns, stables, etc., are very close to the main house, though they are entirely out of sight.

In the plan, smoothly-curved walks are drawn in the thickets of large trees; there is also a vine arbor, which is a handsome ornament. The kitchen garden occupies about one acre and a quarter, and is in proportion to the whole extent of the place.

Fig. 54. Chicken-Coop.

48   WOODWARD'S ARCHITECTURE,

Fig. 55.—A Small Stable.

Valverde, New Mexico............................... 44

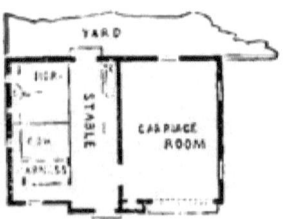

Fig. 56.—Ground Plan.

DESIGN No. 18.

A SMALL STABLE.

BY G. E. HARNEY, ARCHITECT, COLD SPRING, PUTNAM CO., N. Y.

This design for a small stable has accommodation for two horses and a cow, besides a separate apartment for carriages, and another smaller room for harnesses, etc.

The carriage-room measures 13 feet by 22. Each horse-stall is 5½ feet wide, and 9½ feet long to the rear of the stall partition, or 17 feet to the partition of the carriage-room.

The stalls are provided with cast-iron mangers and iron hay-racks, each secured to opposite corners of the stall. We consider these iron fixtures the best in use, but care should be taken to keep them always coated with some kind of paint, to prevent injury to the horses' mouths in winter, when they are liable to become frosted.

The cow-stall is 4½ feet wide, and is provided with a manger and some suitable fastening apparatus; for the latter, we prefer the ring and chain, though the old-fashioned stanchion is recommended by many.

The floors of the stalls should be laid with smoothly-planed locust joists, slanted toward the gutter just enough to take away the water—say 2 inches in the 9½ feet.

The harness-room is provided with hooks for harness; a closet to keep brushes, soap, oils, medicines, etc., etc., and a small stove to heat water for washing harness, etc.

There is a rain-water cistern, built with brick and cement, in the yard, near the rear of the stable, and this, taking water from the roof, by means of tin conductors, supplies all the water required.

Rain water is much better for stock than spring water. The pump is inside the stable, as will be seen in the plan, and empties into a trough, convenient to which are chests lined with tin, for holding oats and meal, etc.

A ventilating shaft rises from the stable-room to the ventilator shown in the sketch, and this, with the small windows in the head of each stall, provides sufficient circulation of air. In the summer, the doors may be taken off their hinges, and gates with locks substituted in their place. The little windows spoken of are placed *above* the heads of the horses—say 7 feet from the floor, and are opened by means of a pulley and rope.

At the rear of the building, a door opens into a yard inclosed by a high fence; and if there be a desire to make the establishment quite complete, there may be built around this yard a range of buildings for poultry, pigs, etc., and open sheds for wagons and carts.

This stable is built of wood, and covered with vertical boarding and battens; the roof is covered with slate; the doors all have simple hoods as well as the windows; and the glass for the latter we would have set in diamond-shaped panes, which, at a little or no extra expense, heightens wonderfully the artistic effect of such a building as this.

Paint the building a warm cream-color, the eaves, and window-trimmings, and doors considerably darker.

DESIGN No. 19.

PLANS FOR IMPROVEMENT OF GROUNDS.

BY E. A. BAUMANN, RAHWAY, N. J.

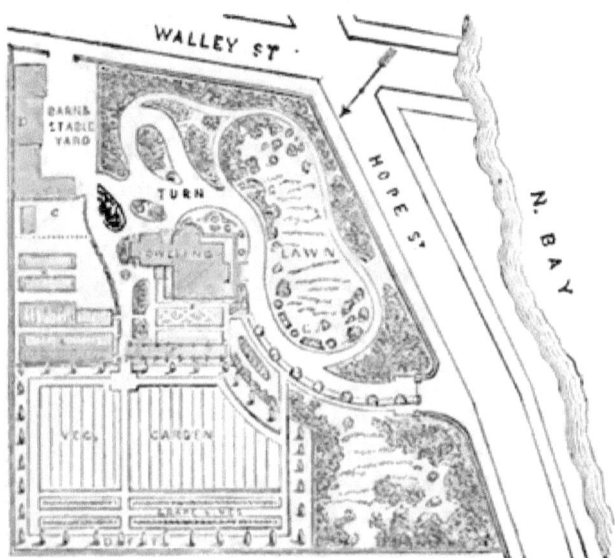

FIG. 57.—PLAN OF FOUR ACRES.

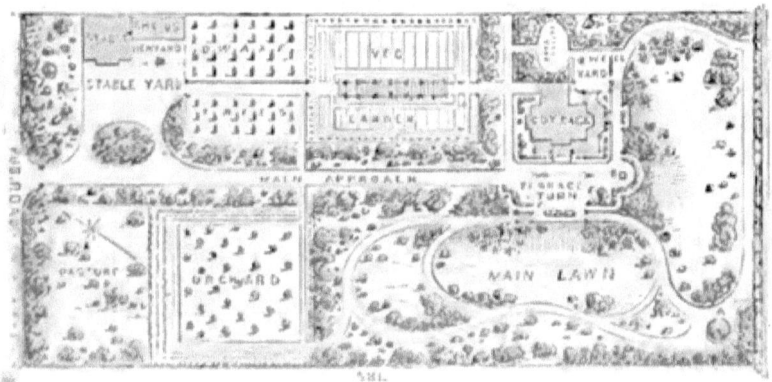

FIG. 58.—PLAN OF FIVE ACRES.

Fig. 59.—Perspective View.

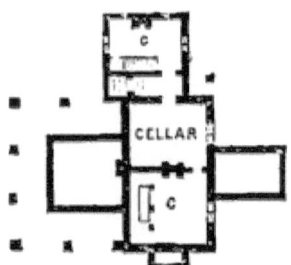

Fig. 60.—Cellar Plan.

Fig. 61.—First Floor.

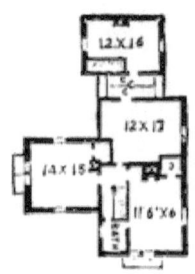

Fig. 62.—Second Floor.

DESIGN No. 20.

We show here a compact, convenient cottage, having a conservatory attached for those who love to gratify their taste for flowers. Each room has a cross draft, and can be abundantly ventilated in warm weather. A passage between the kitchen and dining-room cuts off the smell of cooking, and the doors from the kitchen are double, with spring-hinges, and without locks or other fastenings; they are opened with the foot, and close immediately after passing. The servant can pass in the kitchen through one door and out through the other with a large tray of dishes, and thus avoid meeting any one, while flies and the aroma of cooking have little chance of getting into the main part of the house. We think during the summer months it adds much to the comfort of all country houses to put in the windows the neat, modern wire-gauze window-guard, which does not obstruct air or sight, and does keep out effectually flies, millers, gnats, beetles, spiders, mosquitoes, bats, cats, and the whole list of nuisances against which we make our rooms close and dismal, and mope in summer evening darkness to avoid. The safety, cleanliness, and comfort of an open country house, night and day, can thus be enjoyed; light, sunshine, and fresh air can be had in abundance, and a feeling of comfort insured which those who have once tried it would never be without.

Fig. 63.—Porter's Lodge.

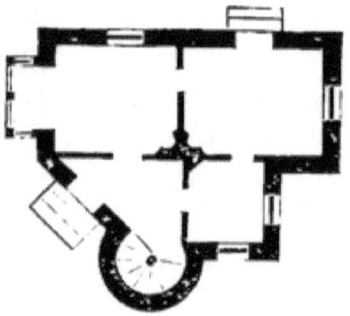

Fig. 64.—Ground Plan.

DESIGN No. 21.

PORTER'S LODGE.

BY GEO. E. HARNEY, COLD SPRING, N. Y.

This design represents a porter's lodge, built about a year ago by Mr. F. P. James, and situated near the gates at the entrance to his country place in Cold Spring.

It is constructed of rough stone, quarried in the immediate vicinity, laid in its natural bed, and pointed up afterward with light-colored mortar, and—though we object to the use of this light mortar, preferring the softer tint of the dark—the effect of the whole is very good, the bright green foliage of the trees, by which it is nearly hidden, contrasting well with the dark gray tone of the stone.

Its walls are low, and its roof projecting boldly, covered with slates cut in an ornamental pattern. The tower, which is the principal feature of the exterior, rises from the angle of the front nearest the public road, and contains the stairways to the chamber and cellar.

The plan shows four apartments on the principal floor, as follows:

The hall is approached by two or three steps, leading to a wide porch, covered with a broadly projecting hood, supported on heavy brackets. This hood is, in fact, a continuation of the roof of the main house beyond the eaves, as is also the roof of the bay window on the adjoining side.

The staircase in the tower is on the right of the front door, and is separated by an archway from the hall.

The room on the left, containing the bay window, is the living-room, and measures 11 feet 6 inches by 13 feet. It opens into a room 15 feet by 11 feet 6 inches, and is used as a kitchen. The other room is a bedroom, and measures 8 feet by 9 feet. The kitchen has a door communicating with the yard in the rear.

The chimney is in the center of the house, and one stack of three flues answers for all the rooms.

There are ventilators on the roof, and a dormer window to light the attic, which has one room finished off for a sleeping-room. All the principal windows are glazed with diamond-shaped panes of glass.

There is a cellar under the whole house, containing bins for coal, store-closets, etc., etc.

Fig. 65.—Well-House.

DESIGN No. 22.

A BARN.

Fig. 66.—A Barn.

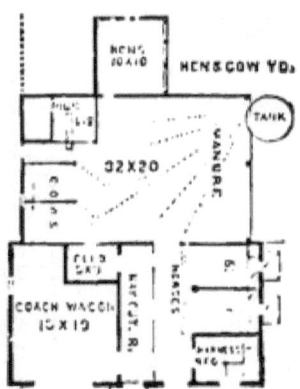

Fig. 67. Ground Plan.

Fig. 68.—A Parsonage.

Fig. 69.—Cellar Plan.

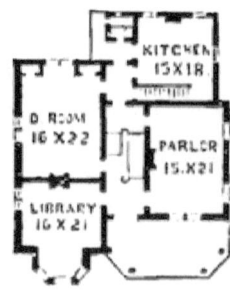

Fig. 70.—First Floor.

Fig. 71.—Second Floor.

DESIGN No. 23.

A PARSONAGE HOUSE.

This design was made for a parsonage house, to be erected in one of the immediate suburbs of New York, and is more commodious than any plan we have thus far shown. The frame to be of the balloon style, sheathed with rough hemlock boards, and covered with narrow siding; roof to be slate, laid in alternate bands of different colors, the lower band to have square ends, the next hexagonal, then square, and so on alternately to the ridge; or shingles may be cut and laid in the same manner. To the top of the first-floor beams the frame should be filled in with brick, to keep out the rats; and if the whole lower floor be grouted between the beams, it would be better and warmer. This is often done to prevent the foul air rising from the cellar through the house. No cellar, however, ought to be foul; ventilate and purify it always; do not have any decaying vegetation in it; grout the floor of the cellar, whitewash the walls and ceiling, and let one open shaft of the chimney start from the cellar. It can be, and should be, at all times sweet and clean. Flooring one inch wide pine; casings, baseboards, etc., to be narrow, neat, and plain; doors 1½ inches in thickness, four paneled; and all interior wood-work to be stained and varnished—not painted. Exterior to be light cream color, with rich, dark-brown trimmings. About New York this house can be erected for $5,000 at present prices of materials and labor.

Fig. 72.

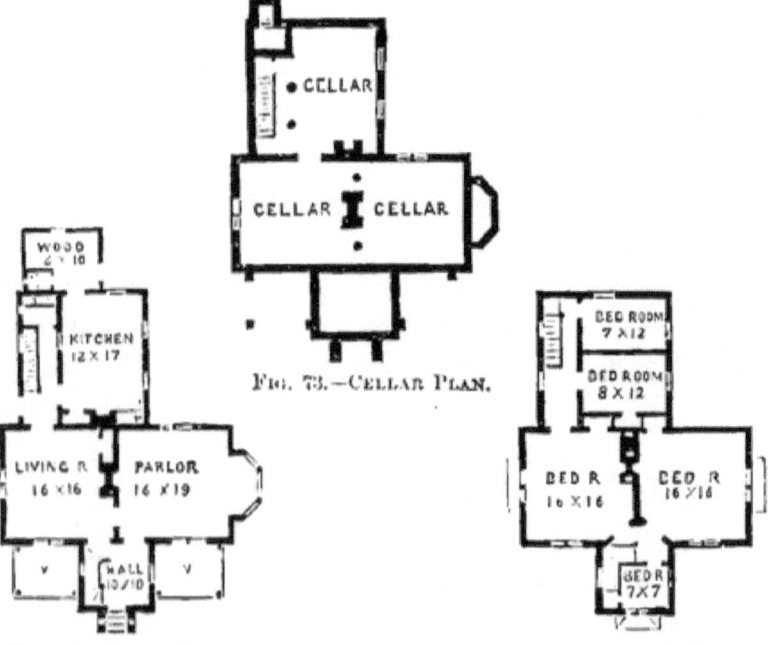

Fig. 73.—Cellar Plan.

Fig. 74.—First Floor.

Fig. 75.—Second Floor.

DESIGN No. 24.

This design, with a tower, adds a variety to our series, and, in many localities, would be suitable and attractive. The plan shows but moderate accommodation, yet enough to supply the demand called for by the largest number. The roof of the main building can be shingled, but that of the tower would be better of tin. It is shown as a frame house, but would look well constructed of brick; hollow walls, one foot thick; but do not omit furring out. We think there is quite as much need of leaving a vacant space between the plastering and a hollow brick wall as if the wall were solid. The brick which binds a hollow wall will convey dampness, though not as much as solid walls. Our designs are mostly shown as being quite low on the ground. There is nothing arbitrary about this, except that it helps the cottage appearance. In many localities custom or prejudice would raise the foundation wall two or even three feet above the ground. There are some places where it would be healthier and better to do so; but on a dry, gravelly soil, or one thoroughly underdrained, we should not care to show more than a foot of underpinning, unless we contemplated making use of rooms below the first floor.

Fig. 76.

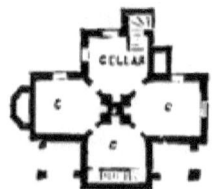

Fig. 77.—Cellar Plan.

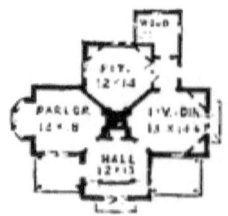

Fig. 78.—First Floor.

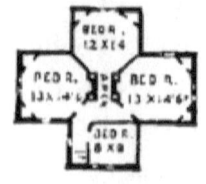

Fig. 79.—Second Floor.

DESIGN No. 25.

This design is quite compact, and can be worked out into a very neat and pretty home, and the rooms changed to suit the exposure. Put the hall on the north side, and a south window can be had in three rooms on the first floor and three rooms on the second floor; and if the kitchen wing be extended, and the kitchen removed back, four rooms can, by sliding doors, be thrown together. The ventilation is very perfect, and each room would command good views. For a summer residence, where every breeze is desirable, this would be a good plan; and it is good for many other reasons; it is easily heated, and the housework can be done with few steps.

In the exterior we give, by way of variety, the hipped or truncated gable, a style of finish we do not very much admire, but which will sometimes answer where there is not a disposition to do too much of it. We call to mind a suburban district where one or two leading citizens introduced this notion when it was less common than now, and the fashion thus set has been persistently followed, until it has become quite a disagreeable feature. Make the gables pointed, and this design, both outside and inside, is a good one.

Fig. 80.

Fig. 81.—Cellar Plan.

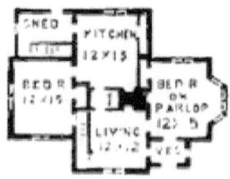

Fig. 82.—First Floor.

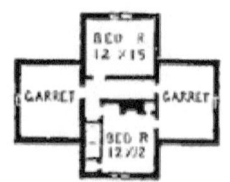

Fig. 83.—Second Floor.

DESIGN No. 26.

Chimneys are an important feature in the exterior design of a dwelling; and we like to see them treated boldly—good solid base, shaft, and projections, and of sufficient height above the roof as to overlook all other obstructions, and thus insure a good draft. The flimsy stovepipe look of chimney-pots we do not admire, and would prefer not to make use of them. A well-built brick chimney can be put up cheaper, and is much more effective.

In this cottage considerable exterior ornamentation is shown, which may be omitted by those who do not like so much of it. The finials and crest on the roof help the appearance very much, and make a good finish; the drapery on the cornice may be plainer. Hoods over the windows, to some extent, take the place of outside blinds, and relieve, by their shadows, what might otherwise appear to be a very plain exterior.

The rooms, as shown on the plan, would probably be better if increased in size; though, if one undertakes to build low-priced houses, and he must adhere firmly to the plan, a little here and a little there will, when all bills are paid, be found to double the cost.

Fig. 84.

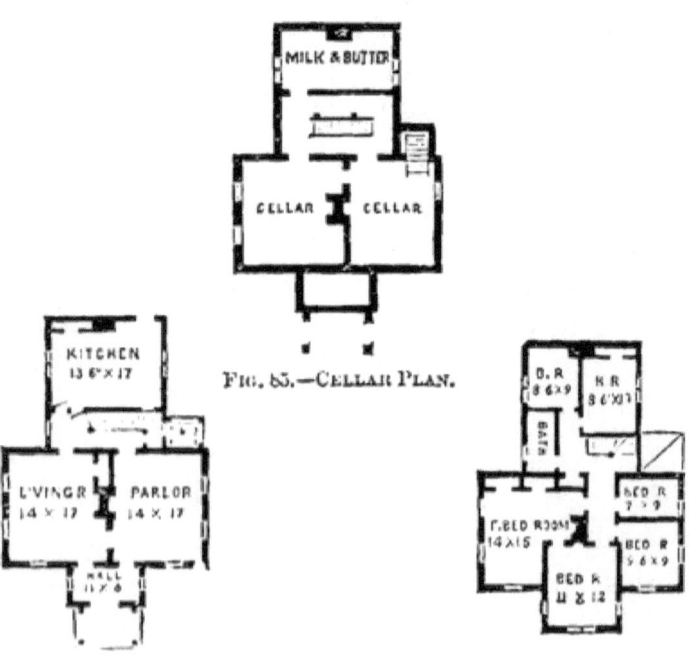

Fig. 85.—Cellar Plan.

Fig. 86.—First Floor.

Fig. 87.—Second Floor.

DESIGN No. 27.

We show here a plain exterior, with a somewhat flatter roof, and full ceilings on the second floor. The bedrooms are all small, and it would probably be better to have a less number, and make them larger, making two rooms out of the four smallest. This roof is what is called one quarter pitch, which is about the flattest that will answer for shingles.

A new roofing material has lately been introduced, called the Mastic Slate, and is highly spoken of by those who have had opportunities to try it. Slate is ground to powder and mixed with gas-works tar, and after being spread with a brush or trowel, becomes in time a sheet of slate. For roofing, it is spread on felting or roofing paper, and the whole expense is very moderate. Our own experience with cheap roofing materials has been quite unsatisfactory, and we have always been glad to exchange them for good tin, shingles, or slate. We would welcome with pleasure the new Mastic Slate, or any other material calculated to reduce the steadily increasing expense of making good, tight, durable roofs. A good material for flat roofs that a farmer can put on himself, is greatly needed.

DESIGNS Nos. 28 and 29.

Fig. 88.—Canopied Seat.

Fig. 89.—A Rustic Seat.

DESIGN No. 30.

Many persons desire to build to meet present wants, and add at future periods such rooms and accommodations as shall be needed for a growing family or are better adapted to the prosperity to which they look forward. Beginning with very small quarters in this way, one has a home early in life and a savings-bank at the same time, with a double incentive to take care of his surplus earnings. He who begins in this way, and is determined to succeed, will succeed, and gradually become the possessor of a neat and comfortable home, without any greater expenditure than that yearly made by a city tenant for accommodations not any more convenient. It has been well said, "We can not all live out of cities (though it were better for all that many more did so); but even the young merchant, lawyer, doctor, mechanic, or clerk, who feels constrained to live on a paved street, might advantageously own a bit of land, though miles away. Travel is rapid and cheap; a day in the country is health and happiness; and we nearly all hope to live in the country by-and-by. With an acre or more of good land well fenced, the habitual plodder over pavements may plant in youth or early prime the trees that are to solace his old age; may have his plants, shrubs, vines, and fruits growing, though unable as yet to build a house—may have an occasional foretaste of the calm joys of living his own master in his own home. No one can realize all the blessedness which centers in home until he comes to have a spot that is truly his own.

"Thousands live and die tenants and hirelings who might far better employ and house themselves. The city hireling makes more money than his country cousin; but strikes and panics, sickness and frolics, with the necessity of giving half he earns for shelter, generally keep him poor; and an increasing family soon drives him to close calculations and shabby shifts to keep afloat. Happy for him and his, for those he takes with him and those he leaves behind, the day that sees him settled in his own cottage, the owner and occupant of a genuine home!"

Fig. 90.

In fig. 90 we show about the simplest form of a house, containing two rooms, as shown in plans figs. 91, 92.

Fig. 91.—First Floor.   Fig. 92.—Second Floor.

In fig. 93 a simple lean-to addition has been made, and this answers for a kitchen, the plan of which is shown in fig. 94.

Fig. 93.

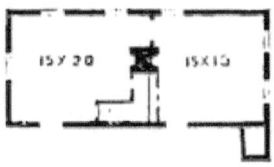

Fig. 94.

In fig. 95 we show the next change, which increases the accommodation and adds to the exterior effect. The plan is shown in fig. 96.

Fig. 95.

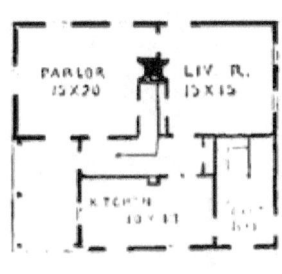

Fig. 96.

72   WOODWARD'S ARCHITECTURE,

Fig. 97.

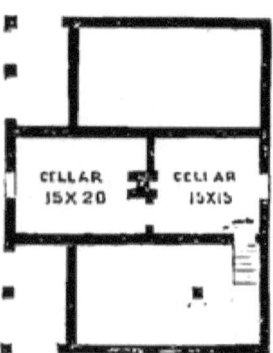

Fig. 98.—Cellar Plan.

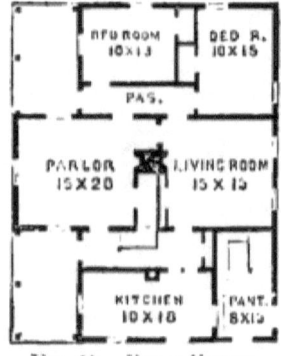

Fig. 99.—First Floor.

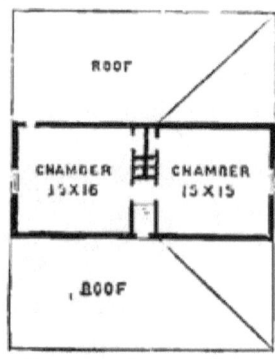

Fig. 100.—Second Floor.

Fig. 97 shows the final arrangement, with pleasant, well-located, and convenient rooms, and an attractive and pleasing exterior.

Figs. 98, 99, and 100 show the plans as finished — a comfortable home, representing, we will say, what during ten years past might otherwise have gone into a landlord's pocket; and independent of this saving, there has been an annual increase in value, now double the entire expenditure. Time, in its many changes, adds beauty and value to a country home that is taken care of, whose occupants enjoy and are interested in every tree and shrub, and every improvement that is made. Fruits, flowers, and ornamental foliage develop new attractions; and a little done to-day, and a little to-morrow, while being but healthful recreation, amounts to a good deal at the end of a year.

Fig. 101.—Design for a Fountain.

74   WOODWARD'S ARCHITECTURE,

Fig. 102.—Suburban Cottage.

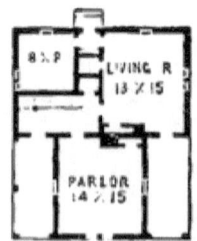

Fig. 103.—First Floor.

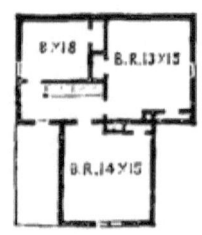

Fig. 104.—Second Floor.

DESIGN No. 31.

A SUBURBAN COTTAGE.

BY GEO. E. HARNEY, ARCHITECT, COLD SPRING, N. Y.

WE show here a design for a small cottage, such as one might build on a village lot of sixty or a hundred feet in width. It is of frame, filled in with brick—soft brick, laid on edge in mortar—and covered with vertical boarding and battens, or with narrow horizontal siding; the roof covered with shingles cut in patterns; the cellar of rubble-stone; the wall 20 inches thick, laid in mortar.

The frame is of spruce or hemlock (the former is the best, but the latter is the most generally used in this part of the country), and the outside finish of white pine—the details few and simple, but bold and strong—everything meaning something, and telling its own story. The roof is quite steep, and the projection of the eaves broad, to shield the sides, and the windows are all wide and airy.

The accommodation of the house is as follows: A veranda, 6 feet wide, shielding the front entrance. The hall, containing the staircases to the chambers and cellar, and opening into the several rooms on this floor. Parlor, 14 feet by 16, communicating by French casement windows with the veranda on one side, and with an open gallery on the other side, and having, besides, a large hooded mullioned window in the front. This room has, also, what we consider indispensable in a country house, be it large or small—an old fashioned open fire-place, for burning wood on the hearth, if wood can be had, or, if not, coal in the grate, and, besides, for purposes of ventilation. We think, for practical reasons, the old poetic sentiment of the family fireside and the blazing log should not be lost sight of, and there should be at least one room in every house—the room that is the most used by the family as a sitting-room—made attractive and healthy by this means.

The living-room, measuring 13 feet by 15, is provided with two good closets, and opens into a little pantry, which is fitted up with a sink and pump, and other pantry conveniences. This opens out upon a stoop to the yard. There is also on this floor a room 8 feet square, which may be used either as a bed-room or as a store-room; it has no chimney, though if one were added, as easily might be, it could be used as an outer kitchen or scullery.

There is a cellar under the whole house, reached by stairs under the main flight. It is provided with a rain-water cistern, bins for coal, and the other usual cellar conveniences of lock-up—cold cellar, hanging shelves, etc. It has a separate entrance of stone steps from the yard, and is 7 feet high in the clear.

In the second story are chambers corresponding severally with the rooms below, and each supplied with a closet. There is no attic, but an opening in the ceiling of the hall communicates with the vacant space above the rooms, and into it ventilates the house, this space having ventilators under the peaks of the gables.

The front chamber has some importance given to it by the addition of an oriel window, after the fashion of some old English cottages—a feature which adds greatly to the brightness of the room, as well as giving some extra space. It is fitted up with a seat, and has glass windows on its three sides.

The interior of this cottage should be fitted up in simple manner with pine; the closets all supplied with shelves, and hooks, and drawers; and the pantry with sink and other fixtures. The walls may have a hard-finished surface, unless it be contemplated to paper them, in which case a cheaper covering can be used.

The inside wood-work may be stained in two shades with umber and oil; and to add to the effect, the finish for the *best* rooms may be of selected stock, so that the finest and best grained wood may be there used.

The outside should be painted three coats of some neutral colors of oil paint—say light browns, or drabs, or grays. The heights of the stories are 9 feet each. The posts are 14 feet long between sill and plate.

Fig. 105.—Hitching Post.

DESIGN No. 32.

PLAN FOR LAYING OUT A LOT ONE HUNDRED FEET BY TWO HUNDRED FEET.

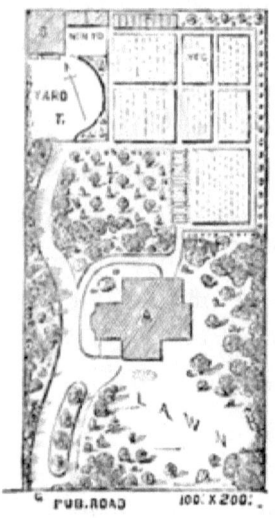

FIG. 106.

A, House.
B, Stable.
T, Turn in Yard.
D, Hot-beds.
H, Grape Arbor.
F, Dwarf and standard fruit-trees.
G, Entrance Gate.
Small fruits in outside border of Vegetable Garden.

DESIGN No. 33.

A TOOL-HOUSE, ETC.

Fig. 107.

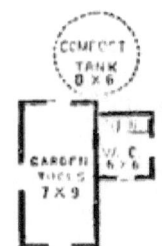

Fig. 108.—Plan.

DESIGN No. 34.

A PIGGERY.

Fig. 109.

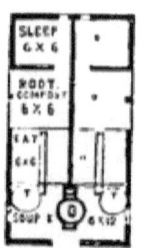

Fig. 110.—Plan.

This is divided lengthwise through the center, so as to divide different breeds, or young pigs from older ones.

DESIGN No. 35.

SMOKE-HOUSES.

Fig. 111.

Fig. 112.

Fig. 113.—Section.

In fig. 112 the fire is designed to be built in the rear building. The fire is built under a flat stone, to spread the smoke; and the earth on the top of the stone prevents it from radiating heat, as shown in section, fig. 113.

DESIGN No. 36.

PLAN FOR LAYING OUT FIVE ACRES FOR A SUBURBAN VILLA.

BY E. FERRAND, DETROIT. MICH.

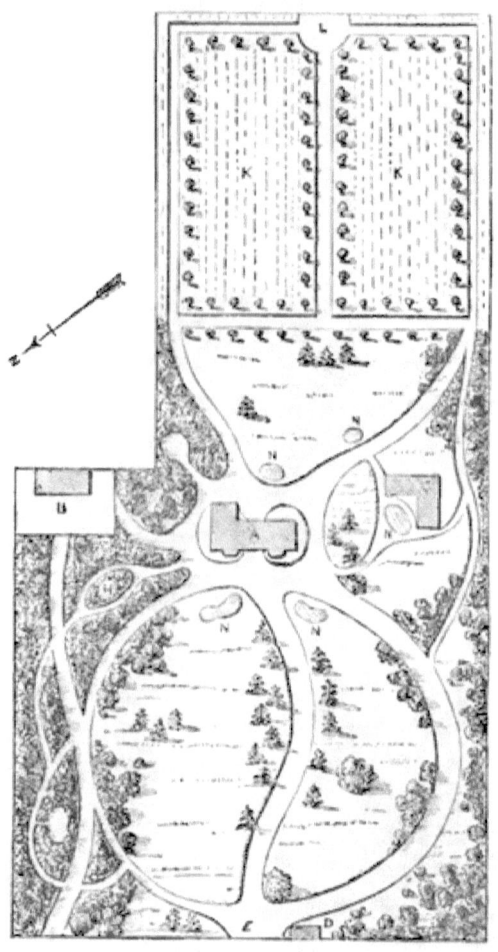

FIG 114.—PLAN.

A, House.
B, Coach-house, Stable, Yard.
C, Greenhouse and Grapery.
D, Gardener's Cottage.
E, Principal Entrance.
F, Entrance to Barn.
H, Group of Rhododendrons and [Azaleas.
K, Kitchen Garden.
L, Entrance on Street.
N, Flower-beds.

In this plan, the kitchen garden occupies about 1½ acres.

DESIGN No. 37.

PLAN FOR LAYING OUT AND EMBELLISHING A LOT SEVENTY-FIVE FEET BY ONE HUNDRED AND FIFTY FEET.

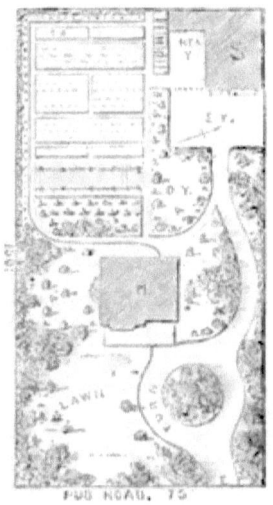

Fig. 115.

H, House.
S, Stable.
A, Fruit-trees on Lawn.
D Y, Drying-yard.
F, Flowers.
S B, Strawberries on the four corners of garden plot.
H B, Hot-beds.

Fig. 116.

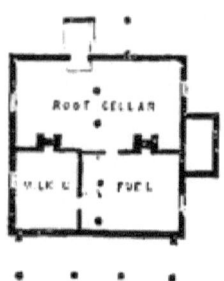

Fig. 117.—Cellar Plan.

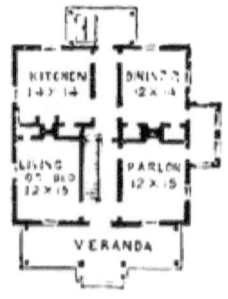

Fig. 118.—First Floor.

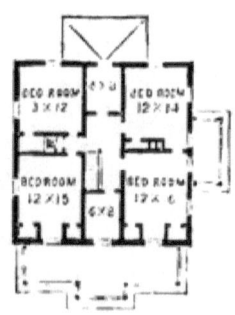

Fig. 119.—Second Floor.

DESIGN No. 38.

We show in this design a square house, with the flat or Italian roof, which, for the amount of room obtained, is probably as cheap a style as can be adopted. Projections should all be treated boldly. The location of the house is oftentimes of great importance. It is difficult to persuade those who live in unfrequented districts to place their dwellings back from the road, the passing vehicle or traveler being too acceptable a sight for those who seldom see any one to disturb the loneliness of their situation. In more thickly populated districts this feeling ceases, and a degree of privacy is wished for. As a matter of taste it is better to have a broad and roomy foreground between the house and the street. It gives a finer effect to the house, an opportunity for display in flowers and ornamental trees, greater freedom from noise and dust, and a moderate amount of seclusion.

The great charm of a country home in pleasant weather is its surroundings, and these should always be neatly kept. Roll and cut the lawn regularly; keep the roads and walks in smooth and handsome order; have fine trees, and give them abundant room to grow, and thin out whenever they become crowded. Do not have any more lawn or roadway or walks than can be kept in unexceptionable order. Whatever is done, do well. Better a city lot in fine order than a one-hundred-acre slovenly farm.

Fig. 120.—A Doctor's Residence.

Fig. 121.—Ground Plan.

DESIGN No. 39.

A DOCTOR'S RESIDENCE.

BY G. E. HARNEY, ARCHITECT, COLD SPRING, N. Y.

This design was built about two years ago, by Dr. P. C. Parker, of Cold Spring, and is situated on a fine piece of ground near and overlooking the village, and embracing beyond fine views of the Hudson, West Point, the Newburgh Gap, and the ranges of mountains above and below.

The house stands between the approach road and the river, consequently the entrance porch is on one front— that toward the road—the living apartments and veranda are on the opposite side, fronting the river; by this means greater privacy is given to those portions of the house usually occupied by the family.

The arrangement of the plan is as follows:

The front veranda, No. 17, opens by wide doors into a vestibule, No. 1, 7 feet square; No. 2 is the hall, containing the staircases, and No. 3 is a small room or recess, opening by means of a French window upon the principal veranda, which extends around the river side of the house. The hall and recess are separated from the main hall by Gothic arches with ornamental columns and molded spandrels; No. 4 is the Doctor's business office, which has a separate entrance for persons calling specially on him, seen at No. 5; No. 6 is a comfortable little library, furnished with book-cases, and having an ornamental chimney-piece; it has two windows, which give pleasant north and west views; No. 7 is a parlor, about 16 feet square, exclusive of the bay window, which projects from its western side about 5 feet, and around which the veranda extends; No. 8 is the dining-room, 15 feet by 16; and No. 9 is a small butler's pantry, fitted up with shelves and cupboards, and opening into the kitchen, No. 11. The kitchen is in the southern wing, and is furnished with sink and other kitchen conveniences; No. 10 is a scullery, fitted up with cupboards and a sink, and supplied with hot and cold water; the dishes are washed here, and passed into the butler's pantry through a small opening left for that purpose in the wall between them, and on a level with the wide shelf of the pantry. A door from the kitchen opens out upon a private veranda, No. 13, which is entirely shut in by lattice-work, and this is used in summer as a laundry or washing-room; No. 14 is the outside stairway of stone, leading to the cellar; and No. 15 is a water-closet, made in a hollow space between two walls, and ventilating through this space into a flue of the kitchen chimney, running along by the side of the kitchen flue. The warmth of the kitchen flue produces a current of air in the ventilating flue, and by this means the water-closet is fully ventilated, and though quite near the house, is always cleanly and inoffensive. Private stairs from the kitchen lead to the chamber floor and to the cellar. The cellar has a laundry under the kitchen, a large store-room under the butler's pantry, and an open cellar under the rest of the house, where are the brick cistern, the furnace, coal-bins, wine-closet, and other conveniences usually found in this portion of the house.

In the second story are two square chambers, with full ceilings, over the parlor and dining-room; two rooms for servants, besides a bathing-room over the kitchen; and a stairway to an unfinished attic over the central portion of the house; a chamber over the library, and a large linen room over the office; all these rooms are well lighted and well supplied with closets.

The house is built of wood, filled in with brick, and sided with narrow pine siding; the roofs throughout, including the window hoods, are all covered with slate, put on in alternate bands of green and purple. The interior walls and ceilings are hard-finished, and the interior woodwork is stained and oiled—three different shades being used for the staining — dark umber, light umber, and annatto. The exterior is painted three different shades of oil paint—of browns and grays—and the doors are grained like oak and walnut. The rooms in the principal story are 10 feet high, and those in the chambers are 9 feet high.

Fig. 122.—Design for a Well-House.

DESIGN No. 40.

ICE-HOUSE, COOLING-ROOM, TOOL-HOUSE, AND WORKSHOP COMBINED.

In this design, the ice is placed in the second story of the main building. The drainage from the ice cools the room below, in which are to be placed meats, fruits, butter, etc. One wing is for a tool-house for farm and garden tools, the other for a workshop. The section is taken lengthwise through the center.

Fig. 123.

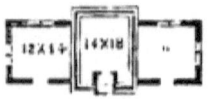

Fig. 124.—Plan.

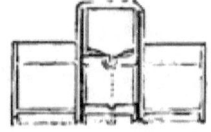

Fig. 125.—Section.

DESIGNS Nos. 41 AND 42.

PLAN FOR LAYING OUT A LOT FIFTY FEET BY ONE HUNDRED AND FIFTY FEET.

Fig. 126.

H. House.
E, Entrance.
O, Hot-beds.
D, Dwarf fruit-trees.
G, Grape trellis.
Vegetable Garden in four square plots.

PLAN FOR LAYING OUT AN IRREGULAR PLOT.

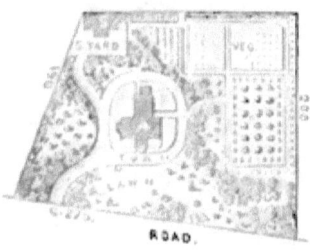

Fig. 127.

A. House. S, Stable, etc., at one end of which is Hot-bed. O, Orchard.

Fig. 128.

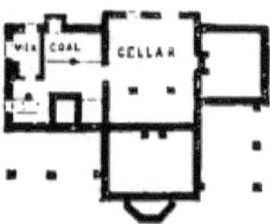

Fig. 129.—Cellar Plan.

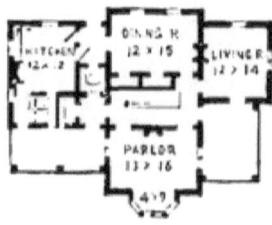

Fig. 130.—First Floor.

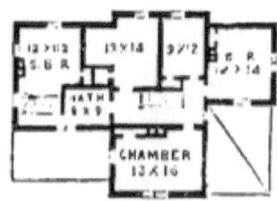

Fig. 131.—Second Floor.

DESIGN No. 43.

A DIFFERENCE of opinion has, and probably always will exist about the materials of which a house should be constructed. We use in this country three leading varieties, wood, brick, and stone, and, to a limited extent, grout and iron. Wood is the cheapest, and if very nice points are considered, is probably the healthiest, certainly the driest. Frame houses have also superior qualities for ventilation, a subject very little understood by those who advocate impenetrable walls and double windows. So little progress has been made in understanding the subject of ventilation, that the commissioners, in advertising for plans for the new Capitol building for the State of New York, mention the necessity of open fire-places for this purpose. Our stone and brick houses, with slate and metal roofs, furnace-heated and air-tight, lack essential qualities for health; while a frame-house, which admits the air more freely, even if it take an extra cord or two of wood, or an extra supply of coal, has a more healthy atmosphere.

Frame houses are good houses, and will outlast the lifetime of the builder; and no matter how strong and substantial a house may be built, it usually passes into strangers' hands at the owner's death.

DESIGN No. 44.

A CHICKEN HOUSE.

Fig. 132.

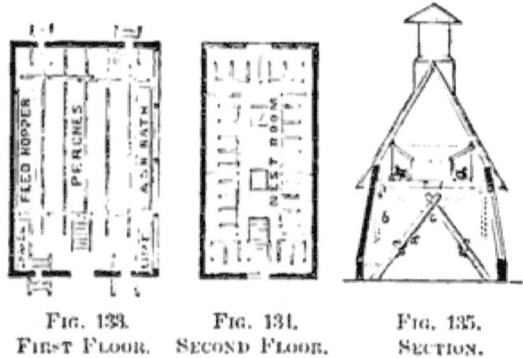

Fig. 133. Fig. 134. Fig. 135.
First Floor. Second Floor. Section.

The perches to be laid back against the walls when cleaning out.

DESIGN No. 45.

PLAN FOR LAYING OUT A LOT ONE HUNDRED AND FIFTY FEET BY TWO HUNDRED FEET.

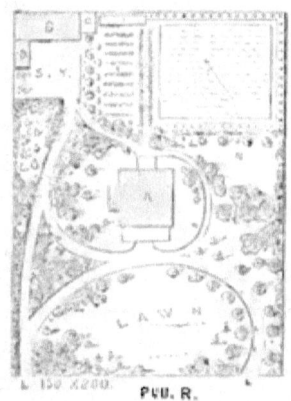

Fig. 136.

A, House.
B, Stable.
D, Henery.
C, Manure Pit.
S Y, Stable Yard.
H, Hot-beds.
G, Dwarf fruit.
N, Drying-yard.
F, Raspberries, along one side of which is a grape arbor covering the walk.
I I, Entrances.
   Currant and other small fruits around outside border.

DESIGN No. 46.

A BARN.

Fig. 137.

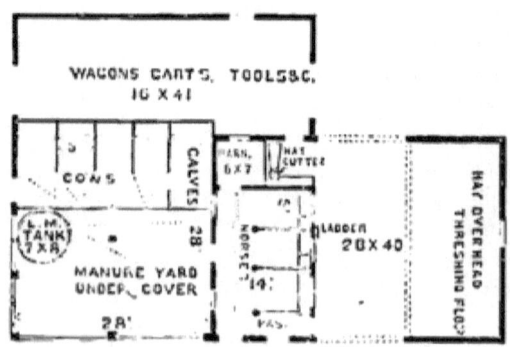

Fig. 138.—Plan.

DESIGN No. 47.

PLAN FOR LAYING OUT A PLOT OF ABOUT TWO ACRES.

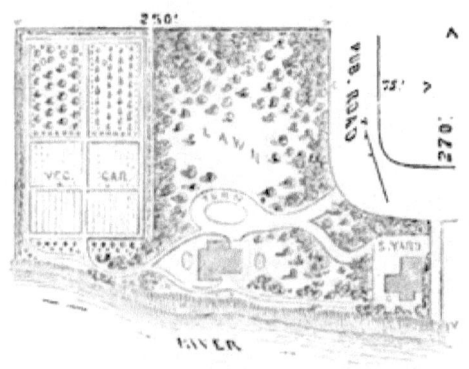

Fig. 139.

H, House.
S, Stable, etc.
C, Hen Yard.
O, Standard Fruits.
D, Dwarf Fruits.
    Blackberries all around the garden.
    Currants, etc., around fruit plots.

DESIGN No. 48.

HOW TO REMODEL AN OLD HOUSE.

Fig. 140.—The Old House.

Fig. 141.—Cellar Plan.

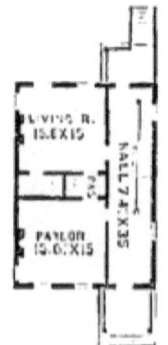

Fig. 142.—First Floor.

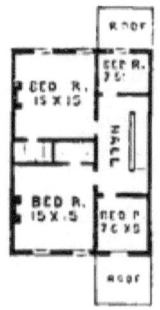
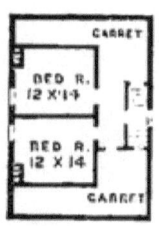

Fig. 143.—Second Floor.   Fig. 144.—Garret.

We show here what can be done with an old house—one built by a retiring citizen, and modeled after his city residence, under the impression, perhaps, it was equally well adapted for the broad open country. We know of many a one who has saved in this manner architect's fees; but such houses sooner or later become subjects for the architect's skill, and not unfrequently a good thing can be made out of them.

Fig. 140 shows the appearance of the old house and the four plans of basement, first floor, second floor, and garret, as they were originally laid out. It is the same thing a thousand times repeated, in almost every densely populated street; every discomfort of a city house, with the interminable stairways, has been transported to the country.

In fig. 145 we show the new design for modernizing, in a tasteful manner, this clumsy exterior. By an addition we give more room upon the two principal floors, so that even a moderate-sized family may abandon, for their own

Fig. 145.—The Old House Remodeled.

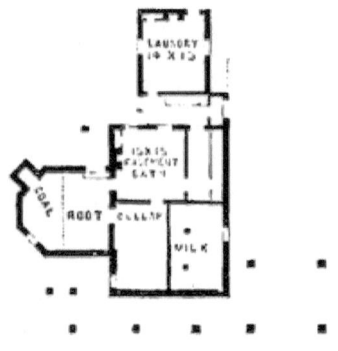

Fig. 146.—Cellar Plan.

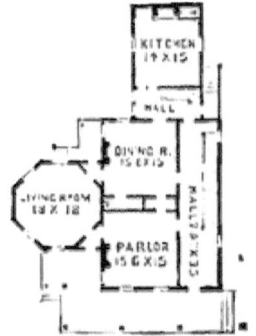

Fig. 147.—First Floor.

 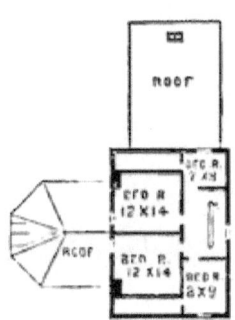

Fig. 148.—Second Floor.　　　Fig. 149.—Garret.

use, both basement and garret. A broad and spacious veranda, with *porte cochere* at one end, adds greatly to the outside enjoyment and appearance, and the exterior outline and shadow so managed as to make a pleasing impression. The grounds and other surroundings have also been differently planned; a handsomely curved line of roadway takes the place of the straight-line communication with the highway. The orchard of apple-trees which surrounds the house will be thinned out and planted up with ornamental trees, thus breaking up the parallel lines. The lawn in front is to be kept smooth, clean, and handsome, and all the awkward stiffness of house, grounds, and shrubbery changed to the graceful ease of an inviting country house with a neat and spacious foreground. All this is accomplished with a small expenditure of money, which, however, might have been saved on the start by one wise enough to employ the proper talent to aid him in the design.

DESIGN No. 49.

PLAN FOR LAYING OUT A LOT OF ONE ACRE.

Fig. 150.

S, Stable and Barn.
A, Greenhouse and Grapery.
O, Double Henery.
H, Hen Yard, set with fruit-trees.
D, Grape Arbor, between which and Greenhouse is a row of dwarf fruit-trees.
I, Dwarf and Standard fruit-trees and currants.
F, Fountain.
J, Flowers.
O, Water-closet and Garden Tool-house in rear.
E, Dwarf fruit-trees.

DESIGN No. 50.

PLAN FOR LAYING OUT A LOT OF TWO ACRES.

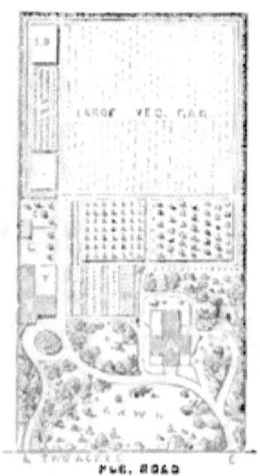

Fig. 151.

A, House.
E, Entrance.
B, Stables and Carriage-house.
D, Greenhouse and Grapery.
I, Henery, with double yard, C C, containing a few fruit-trees.
S B, Strawberries.
R B, Raspberries.
V, Dwarf Orchard.
O, Standard Orchard.
    Grapes between Greenhouse and Stables.
    Surrounding border of Garden set with blackberries.

COMPUTING COST.

A simple and rapid plan for estimating the cost of any building is by comparison. If carefully done, it will give figures that may be relied on. We have said before that it would be productive of much mischief to name prices in a book like this. The only prices we could give would be local ones, and these are changing here every day. We were of this opinion when we prepared "Woodward's Country Homes," a book that has met with extraordinary success, and has been ordered from every quarter of the globe; and experience thus far confirms us in the belief that the opinion then formed was correct.

The best substitute for prices, on which confidence may be placed, is the following, a plan much used by builders to test the accuracy of their detail estimates:

We will suppose that a party desires to erect a building in the vicinity of Madison, Wis., where prices of materials and labor differ largely from New York prices. Let him select such a house already built in that vicinity as shall represent, in style of architecture and character of finish, about what he desires to construct, and of which the cost of building is known; then compute the area or number of square feet covered by the building; divide the number of dollars of cost by the number of square feet thus found, and the price per square foot is ascertained.

Thus a house 40 feet by 40 feet covers an area of 1,600 square feet; it costs $8,000; and dividing $8,000 by 1,600, shows $5 per square foot. Now what will be the cost of a similar house covering 1,400 square feet?

$$1,400 \times \$5 = \$7,000.$$

This plan will do very well to approximate roughly to cost. A better and closer one is to ascertain the cost per cubic foot. Thus, a house 40 feet by 40 feet, and an average height of 30 feet. $40 \times 40 \times 30 = 48,000$ cubic feet, cost $7,200, or fifteen cents per cubic foot. Then a house containing 57,000 cubic feet, at fifteen cents, would cost $8,550. Where all conditions of comparison are equal, such as equal facilities for buying, equal advantages in capital, credit, good management, etc., one can very closely by, this last method, ascertain about the cost of such a building as he proposes to erect.

Fig. 152.—Design for Gateway.

Fig. 153.

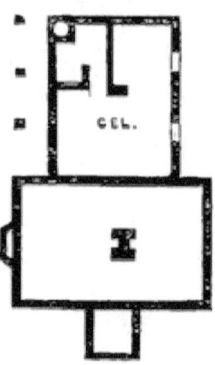

Fig. 154.—Cellar Plan.

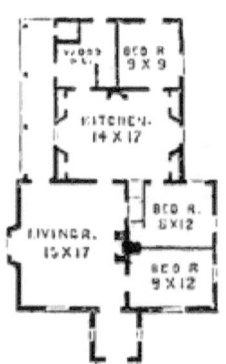

Fig. 155.—First Floor.

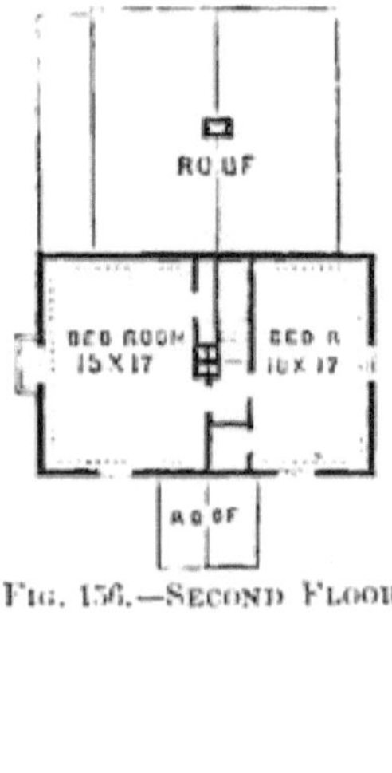

Fig. 156.—Second Floor.

DESIGN No. 51.

This cottage shows a somewhat different construction outside from those already given, and although it adds somewhat to the expense, gives more variety.

Such a plan as this can be added to advantageously whenever desirable to do so. Indeed, most of the plans given admit of additions; and one advantage of the Rural Gothic style is, that every wing put on increases the exterior effect. Add almost anything in keeping with the original structure, let the roofs be on different levels, and the building will assume the appearance of a pile of buildings, irregular in outline and prolific in beauties of light and shadow.

Finish the walls with two coats of mortar and one coat of hard finish; on the lower floor put in a simple cornice, and omit all plaster ornaments. Stain and oil or varnish all interior wood-work; do not paint any room but the kitchen.. In this manner you can get a warm and pleasing effect, and have the wood-work always free from dirt. Good effects can be produced by staining moldings and panels to resemble different varieties of wood; or our native hard woods can be used with fine effect, if expense is not considered. It may not generally be known that all mahogany and rosewood furniture is stained, the natural wood being very much lighter in color.

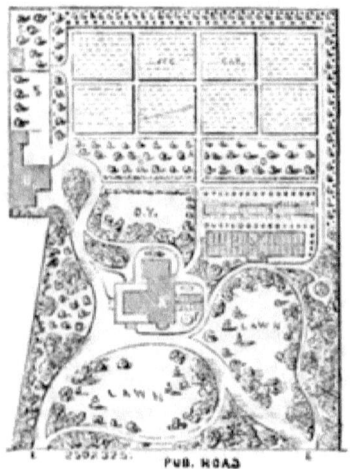

Fig. 157.

    A, House.
    C, Conservatory, side of house.
    B, Stable, Carriage-house, etc.
    D, Henery, with double yard, S S, set in plants.
D Y, Drying-yard.
    G, Grapery and Greenhouse.
    F, Fountain.
E E, Entrance Gates.
    T, Grape Trellis.
O O, Orchard.
        Fruit around garden.

DESIGN No. 52.

PLAN FOR LAYING OUT A LOT TWO HUNDRED AND FIFTY FEET BY THREE HUNDRED AND TWENTY-FIVE FEET.

The lot for which this design was made had one side irregular, as shown, but the planting has been so managed that no one would suspect that such an abruptness existed. Two separate lawns are shown, divided by the carriage drive. The lawns are planted on their outer edges, but are better open and clear from all shrubbery in the interior. They should, throughout the growing season, be closely mown at least every two weeks. The drive from street to house should be 10 feet wide, and finished with a hard, smooth, and evenly graded surface, and kept free from weeds; edges of lawn to be trimmed neatly as often as required. Whatever is done in the way of ornamental grounds should be well done. Nothing looks so shabby as neglected walks and overgrown lawns; better not make any attempt to lay out the grounds tastefully, unless there is a disposition to keep them neat and well ordered. The stable is planted out in such a manner as not to be seen from the house, and the general arrangement of the grounds is such as will make them attractive and convenient. The lot contains about two acres, abundantly large for one whose business is elsewhere. No one need ever be in want of occupation for his leisure hours when he has two acres to embellish and see to its neat keeping.

DESIGN No. 53.

A BARN.

Fig. 158.

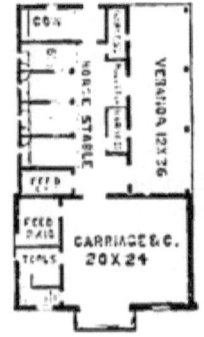

Fig. 159.—First Floor.

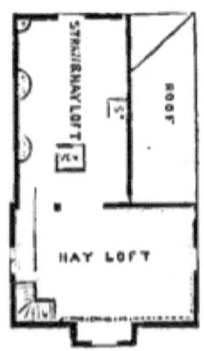

Fig. 160.—Second Floor.

DESIGN No. 54.

A FARM COTTAGE.

Fig. 161.

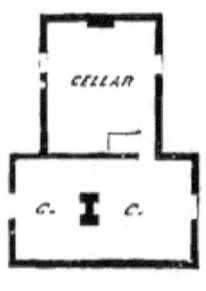

Fig. 162.
Cellar Plan.

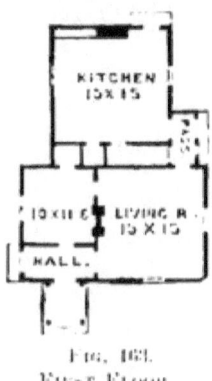

Fig. 163.
First Floor.

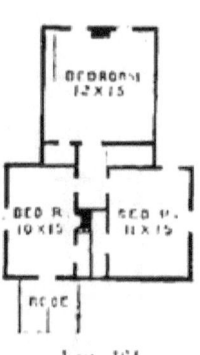

Fig. 164.
Second Floor.

Fig. 165.—A Farm-House.

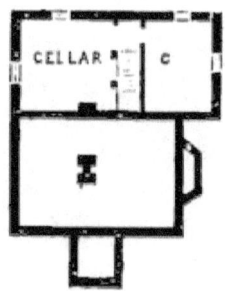

Fig. 166.—Cellar Plan.

Fig. 167.—First Floor.

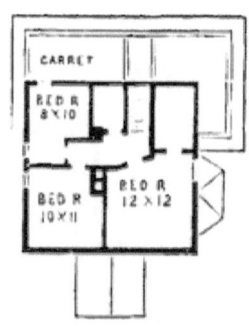

Fig. 168.—Second Floor.

DESIGN No. 55.

A FARM-HOUSE.

This design shows a neat and compact farm-house, covered by a plain roof, without hips or valleys, with a number of conveniently arranged, but not very large, bed-rooms. It must be understood that these designs, in all cases, admit of many changes; that is, rooms may be made larger or smaller, and increased or decreased in number; the exterior in one design may be used for the ground-plan of another, or the good points of several plans may be collected and an entirely new plan re-arranged from them, and an exterior adapted to it. In all designs shown, the perspective view is adapted to the plans connected with it; and in making changes there are many points to be thoroughly considered. In some instances it would be necessary to reverse the plan; that is, change the location of rooms from one side to the other, in order to take advantage of the exposure.

That we should succeed in meeting in all respects the wishes of any one person, we do not expect; yet repeated instances have come to our knowledge of buildings having been put up in exact accordance with our published plans. We believe, however, that we do give every one who contemplates building, suggestions and plans of great value, and one can, with a little ingenuity, adapt the hints to suit his own peculiarities.

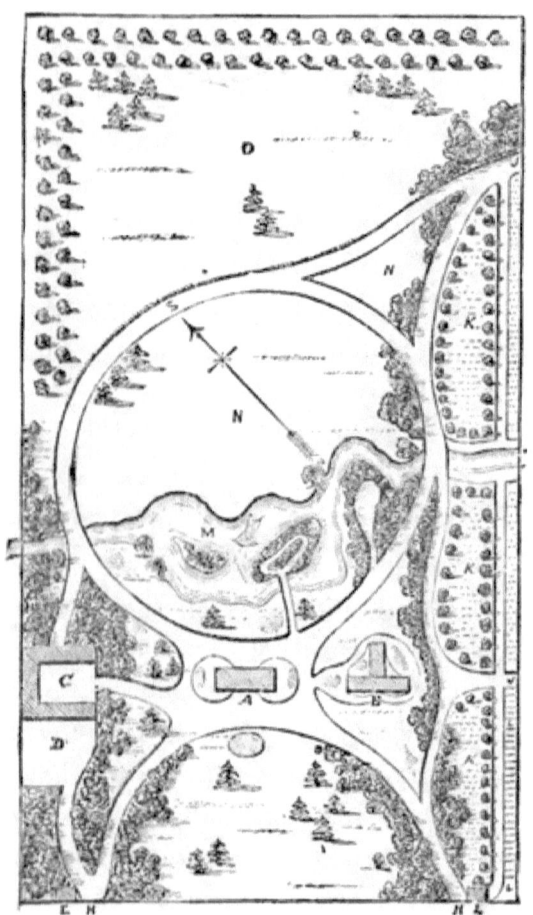

Fig. 169.—Plan.

A, Dwelling.
B, Greenhouses and Graperies.
C, Stable, Barn, and Interior Yard.
D, Yard.
E, F, Gardeners' Houses.
H Principal Entrances.
J, Entrances.
K, Vegetable Garden.
L, Hot-beds.
M, River, Lake, and Islands.
N, Meadow.
O, Fields, with two rows of apple-trees.

DESIGN No. 56.

PLAN FOR LAYING OUT A TEN-ACRE LOT FOR SUBURBAN OCCUPATION.

BY E. FERRAND, DETROIT, MICH.

This place has two main entrances, with well-shaded drives. The lodges for the gardeners command the gates. There is an immediate access from one of these cottages to the hot-beds and garden, which are exposed to the full sun. The sight of the vegetable garden is entirely hidden by a belt of ornamental planting. Around the greenhouse and graperies are flower-beds and rustic seats, with a nice walk around. Rhododendrons and kalmias can be planted on the northern and other shaded sides of the dwelling. The access is very easy to the stables and other out-buildings, with two yards and a direct access to the street. The river and lake occupy about half an acre. There are two islands, one of which is connected with the garden by a small bridge. The space O can be cultivated with fruits of any kind, or put in grass.

It has been my aim to make this a handsome place, with but few roads. In fact, a simple glance at the drawing will tell more about the disposition of this place than any explanation.

Fig. 170.—A School-House.

Fig. 171.—Ground Plan.

DESIGN No. 57.

A COUNTRY SCHOOL-HOUSE.

BY GEO. E. HARNEY, ARCHITECT, COLD SPRING, N. Y.

WE present at this time a sketch of a country school-house, of suitable size and accommodation for about fifty pupils, of both sexes.

It is a plain building of wood, comprising a central portion and two wings, one on each side. The main building measures 21 feet by 42, and the wings 12 by 17 each. The principal school-room measures 20 feet by 30, and is 12 feet high to the spring of the ceiling, and 17 feet high in the center of the room, the ceiling for a portion of the way following the slant of the rafters, and the principal rafters and braces projecting out so as to show from below. The walls of this room are wainscoted up to the level of the window-sills—4 feet from the floor—with narrow ceiling boards, and above that, together with the ceiling, are finished off with a rough and stucco finish.

The wood-work should all be stained, and the walls tinted some soft neutral tint—gray, or cream, or pearl color.

The windows are all sash windows, double-hung for purposes of ventilation; and, in addition, there are two ventilating shafts rising from the floor through the attic, and terminating in the ventilator on the ridge of the main roof. These shafts have openings near the floor and ceiling, with arrangements for opening and shutting at will. They are made of smoothly-planed, well-jointed pine boards, and measure each 16 inches square inside.

In order to keep up the circulation, and to supply cool air from outside, a shaft is introduced running along under the floor, and terminating at the platform on which, in winter, the stove, or heating-apparatus, will stand, and from this distributed into the room by numerous small holes in the riser of the platform.

We consider the simplest methods of ventilation the best, and the above will be found both simple and effective. The great desideratum is to provide means for the discharge of a certain quantity of vitiated air, and to supply its place by the same quantity of pure air, properly warmed in winter. To make the discharge more effective, the stove-pipe may be carried up in connection with one of the shafts, rarefying the air, and making the upward current stronger; but in ordinary cases this will be hardly necessary.

There are two entrances to this house, one for boys and one for girls. Both entries are 10 feet square, and are in the main building, opening directly into the school-room.

The wing on the right is a class-room, and that on the left is designed for wood and coal, and for a wash-room, if such be considered desirable.

The entries, instead of having hooks for clothing, have each a sufficient number of boxes or shelves divided up into compartments of about two cubic feet each, ranged along the sides, and carried up in three or four tiers. These boxes are all numbered, and each scholar has one for his own exclusive use; being provided with a duplicate number as a voucher, there is no opportunity for contention as to ownership, no losing or abusing of hats and shawls, and dinner-pail. The method has been tried, and found much preferable to the old arrangements of hooks, particularly for the smaller scholars, and those coming from a distance who bring their dinners.

The two porticoes measure 8 feet by 10; the windows have all broad hoods and brackets; the gables have heavy finials, and the ridge is surmounted by a large ventilator. The roofs are covered with slates, and the walls are painted two or three coats of oil paint.

Fig. 172.—Design for Entrance Gate.

DESIGN No. 58.—A GRAPE ARBOR.

BY E. A. BAUMANN.

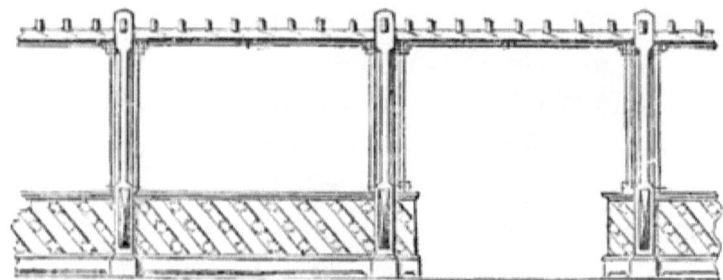

FIG. 173.—SIDE VIEW OF ARBOR.

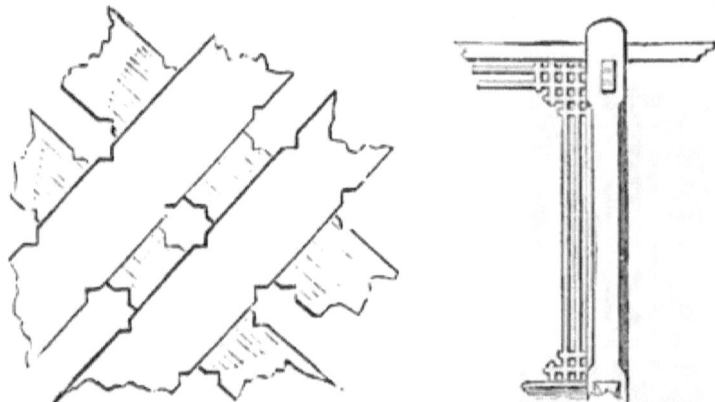

FIG. 174.—DETAIL OF ARBOR.   FIG. 175.—DETAIL OF ARBOR.

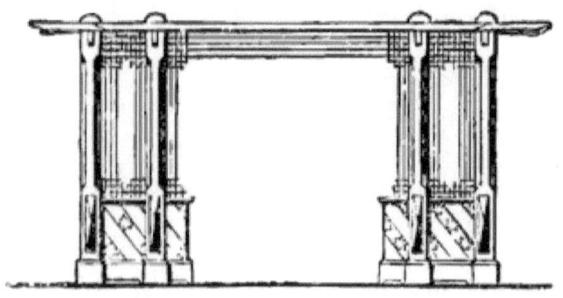

FIG. 176.—CROSS SECTION.

Advertising Sheet, Woodward's Annual.—1867.

EMPIRE STATE GAS MACHINE,

(Levi Stevens' Patents, including Cunningham's Patent,)

For supplying Dwellings, Stores, Factories & Public Buildings.

The Empire State Gas Machine is the most simple and effective means known for producing gas without heat. Its action is automatic, feeding itself with constant supplies of Gasoline, thus securing steady and and uniform supplies of gas.

The gas produced is equal to the best known illuminating gas. It is as economical as any other, and is adapted to a wider range of use for lighting, heating and mechanical purposes.

It will maintain its illuminating power under as great a degree of cold as any other.

It is free from danger with ordinary care in using gas.

Its remarkably pure and steady light is pleasant for the eye.

It renders it easy for persons living remote from street gas pipes to enjoy the luxury of a pure gas light, at a comparatively small cost, and with little trouble.

The public are invited to witness its operation at our Store,

620 BROADWAY, N. Y.

Gasoline may be obtained at market prices from the various sources of supply now in operation. Names of reliable parties manufacturing and shipping the article may be obtained on application to us.

No. 1 supplies 5 Argand Burners.
No. 2   "   10   "   "
No. 3   "   20   "   "
No. 4   "   30   "   "
No. 5   "   50   "   "
No. 6   "   75   "   "
No. 7   "   100   "   "
No. 8   "   250   "   "
No. 9   "   500   "   "

MITCHELL, VANCE & CO.,

MANUFACTURERS OF

Chandeliers, Medieval & Architectural Church Fixtures,

ECCLESIASTICAL EMBLEMS,

And every description of Gas Fixtures, Coal Oil Chandeliers and Lamps, in Metal and Glass; with a complete assortment of Lamp Stands and Trimmings, Glass and Paper Shades, also, manufacturers of Gilt and Bronze Clocks.

WAREHOUSE & SALESROOMS,—620 BROADWAY.

MANUFACTORY,—335, 337, 339, 341 & 343 West 24th St., cor. 10th Ave.

NEW YORK.

FRUIT
AND
ORNAMENTAL TREES
For Fall of 1866.

ELLWANGER & BARRY,

Invite the attention of Planters, Nurserymen and Dealers in Trees, to their extensive stock now offered for the Fall Trade.

In the Departments of

HARDY FRUIT TREES,
ORNAMENTAL TREES,
SHRUBS AND PLANTS,

The Collections are the most Extensive and Complete in the United States.

Prompt and careful attention given to all orders, and packing done in the most skilful and thorough manner.

Full particulars will be found in the following Catalogues, which will be sent, pre-paid, to applicants who enclose stamps:—

Nos. 1 and 2—Ten cents each; No. 3, five cents; No. 4, three cents.

No. 1.—A Descriptive and Illustrated Catalogue of Fruits.

No. 2.—A Descriptive and Illustrated Catalogue of Ornamental Trees, Shrubs, Roses, &c., &c., &c.

No. 3.—A Catalogue of Dahlias, Verbenas, Petunias, and select new Greenhouse and Bedding Plants, published every spring.

No. 4.—A Wholesale Catalogue or Trade List, published every autumn.

ELLWANGER & BARRY,
Mount Hope Nurseries,
ROCHESTER, N.Y.

SING SING GRAPE VINES.

If I should publish all the testimony I have received from my friends and customers, to establish the superiority of my Vines, it would make too large a book. Suffice it to say that those who bought of me in 1863 sent larger orders in 1864, and bought again in 1865; and this year, I am happy to say that my Vines are better than any I have previously grown.

Do you ask why I have always *good Vines?* It is, I believe, because I know how to grow them—because I do nothing but take care of them—and have no other business whatever. I raise nothing but Grape Vines.

It is for these reasons that my Vines are good, and that for the last three years I have not been able to meet the demand; and have had to advertise to keep back new orders.

I must add, also, that I sell only Vines grown by myself. I buy no cheap Vines in other places, to fill up my orders; and hence I know what I sell, and can warrant every Vine in name and quality.

My stock this year is

Iona,
Israella,
Adirondac,
Delaware,
Allen's Hybrid,
Creveling,
Concord, a few **Union Village** and
Rogers' Hybrids, Nos. 4, 15 and 19.

Other varieties in my Catalogue are in small numbers only for the retail trade.

Send for price list or catalogue.

J F. DELIOT, Vine Grower,
SING SING, N. Y.

MINTON'S
ENCAUSTIC
AND
PAVING TILES,

BANKS, CHURCHES,
&c., &c.,

AS LAID BY US IN THE

CAPITOL AT WASHINGTON,

ALSO,

GARNKIRK CHIMNEY TOPS,

AND

PLUMBERS' MATERIALS OF EVERY DESCRIPTION.

FOR SALE BY

MILLER & COATES,

279 PEARL STREET, New York.

BOOKS
FOR
MECHANICS, BUILDERS,
&c., &c.

For sale, or sent post-paid to any address, on receipt of price.

—:o:—

Allen's Rural Architecture	$1 50
Cleveland's Villas and Cottages	4 00
Cummings' Designs for Street Fronts, Suburban Houses and Cottages, with full exterior and interior details, 382 designs and 714 illustrations.—A new work, and the best practical work on modern details yet published; indispensable for those who wish to keep posted on all the latest improvements	10 00
Downing's Cottage Architecture	3 00
Downing's Country Houses	8 00
Hatfield's American House Carpenter	3 50
Leuchar's How to Build and Ventilate Hot-Houses	1 50
Manual of the House, 126 designs and plans..........cloth,	1 50
New Clock and Watch Maker's Manual	2 00
Ready Reckoner	50
Silloway's Modern Carpentry	2 00
Sloan's Homestead Architecture, 200 Engravings	4 00
Sloan's Ornamental Houses, 26 Colored Engravings	3 00
Todd's Young Farmer's Manual	1 50
Vaux's Villas and Cottages; nearly 400 Engravings	3 00
Woodward's Country Homes	1 50
Woodward's Graperies and Horticultural Buildings	1 50
Woodward's Annual of Architecture..........paper, 75c. cloth,	1 00
Art of Saw Filing. Illustrated	75
Boston Machinist. (Fitzgerald)	75
Carpenters' and Joiners' Hand-Book. Illustrated	75

ADDRESS,

GEO. E. & F. W. WOODWARD,
Publishers of Architectural Books,
37 PARK ROW, N.Y.

FIRE ON THE HEARTH!
—:o:—
GEO. E. & F. W. WOODWARD, 37 PARK ROW, N.Y.,
NEW YORK AGENTS FOR
DIXON'S LOW DOWN PHILADELPHIA GRATE
For Burning Wood or Coal, for sale at Manufacturers' Prices.

"It is a plan for warming houses, which has never in all its points been surpassed."

"It is believed that there is scarcely a single educated Physician in Philadelphia who owns the house he lives in, who is not supplied with one or more of these delightful luxuries."

"We have one of these admirable contrivances, put in our house in 1859, and every additional year only increases our appreciation of the luxury."—*Dr. W. W. Hall, Editor of Hall's Journal of Health, N.Y.*

Four sizes and three styles of finish—Japanned, Dead Ground and Polished Steel. Prices range from $35 to $60. *The best and neatest open Parlor or Library Fire. Packed and Shipped to all parts of the country.*

Send for Descriptive Illustrated Circular.

Address, GEO. E. & F. W. WOODWARD,
37 Park Row, New York.

Advertising Sheet, Woodward's Annual.—1867.

THE HOWE SEWING MACHINES,
699 BROADWAY,
Corner Fourth Street,   NEW YORK.
FOR FAMILIES AND MANUFACTURERS.

THE HOWE LOCK STITCH.
THESE WORLD-RENOWNED SEWING MACHINES

Are celebrated for doing the best work, using a much smaller needle for the same thread than any other machine, and by the introduction of the most approved machinery, we are now able to supply the very best machines in the world. These machines are made at our new and spacious Factory at Bridgeport, Conn., under the immediate supervision of the President of the Company, ELIAS HOWE, Jr., the original inventor of the Sewing Machine.

The Stitch invented by Mr. HOWE, and made on this machine, is the most popular and durable, *and all Sewing Machines are subject to the principle invented by him.*

The Howe Machine Company,
699 BROADWAY, cor. Fourth Street, N. Y.

EMPIRE SHUTTLE SEWING MACHINES
ARE SUPERIOR TO ALL OTHERS
FOR FAMILY AND MANUFACTURING PURPOSES.

Contain all the latest improvements; are speedy, noiseless, durable and easy to work. Illustrated Circulars free. Agents wanted. Liberal discounts allowed. No consignments made. Address,

Empire Sewing Machine Company,
616 BROADWAY, New York.

ARCHITECTURAL,
ORNAMENTAL LANDSCAPE AND RUSTIC
DESIGNS, DRAWINGS & PLANS
EXECUTED IN BEST STYLES, BY
E. C. HUSSEY,
Horticulturist Office, Room 7.   **37 Park Row, N. Y.**
Also, DRAWING AND ENGRAVING ON WOOD.

Advertising Sheet, Woodward's Annual.—1867.

PUBLICATIONS OF GEO. E. & F. W. WOODWARD, 37 Park Row, N. Y.

NEW BOOKS—UNIFORM EXTRA CLOTH BINDINGS.

I. **WOODWARD'S ANNUAL of Architecture, Landscape Gardening and Rural Art for 1867.**
Containing 176 original designs and plans of low priced Cottages, Farm-houses, Out-buildings, with plans for laying out and embellishing small plots of ground. 12mo. 120 pages. Cloth, extra, $1.00

II. **FULLER'S FOREST TREE CULTURIST.**
A new work on the propagation, cultivation and management of Forest Trees, by Andrew S. Fuller, author of the Grape Culturist. Fully illustrated, post paid, 12mo. 188 pages, cloth, extra, ..$1.50

III. **GRAPES AND WINE.**
A new and practical work on the Cultivation of the Native Grape and Manufacture of American Wine; by Geo. Husmann, of Missouri. Fully illustrated. 12mo. 192 pages...Cloth, extra, $1.50

IV. **WOODWARD'S COUNTRY HOMES.**
A practical work, with 150 Designs and Plans of Country Houses of moderate cost, with illustrated description of the manner of constructing Balloon Frames. 12mo. 188 pp..Extra binding, $1.50

V. **Woodward's Graperies & Horticultural Buildings.**
A practical work on the Design and Construction of all classes of Buildings for Growing Plants, and Ripening Fruit under glass. 60 illustrations..............12mo. 140 pages. Cloth, extra, $1.50

VI. **WOODWARD'S DELAWARE GRAPE.**
Colored Plate, full size, extra,............................ $3.00

VII. **THE HOUSE.**
A New Manual of Rural Architecture; or, How to Build Dwellings, Barns, Stables and Out-Buildings of all kinds; with a Chapter on Churches and School Houses, by D. H. Jacques..12mo. 176 pp. Cloth, $1.50

VIII. **THE GARDEN.**
A New Manual of Practical Horticulture; or, How to Cultivate Vegetables, Fruits and Flowers; with a Chapter on Ornamental Trees and Shrubs. 12mo. 166 pages...............Cloth, $1.00

IX. **THE FARM.**
A New Manual of Practical Agriculture; or, How to Cultivate all the Field Crops; with an Essay on Farm Management, etc. 12mo. 156 pages...........................Cloth, $1.00.

X. **THE BARN-YARD.**
A New Manual of Cattle, Horse and Sheep Husbandry; or, How to Breed and Rear the various species of Domestic Animals. 12mo. 168 pages ....Cloth, $1.00.
Either of the above sent, post paid, on receipt of price.

Established 1846.

XI. **THE HORTICULTURIST.**
Two Dollars and Fifty Cents per Annum.
A Monthly Magazine devoted to the Orchard, Vineyard, Garden, and Nursery to culture under glass, Landscape Gardening, Rural Architecture, &c. Fully illustrated.

XII. **DE LA VERGNE'S SULPHUR BELLOWS,**
For the Prevention of Mildew and Destruction of Insects,.... $3.50

HOMES FOR THE MILLION!

WOODWARD'S ANNUAL
Of Architecture, Landscape Gardening and Rural Art for 1867.

176 original and practical designs and plans for low-priced
COUNTRY HOMES,
COTTAGES,
FARM HOUSES,
BARNS,
OUT-BUILDINGS,
with numerous plans for laying out small plots of ground. 12mo. 120 pages. Cloth extra, $1.00. Post paid.

WOODWARD'S COUNTRY HOMES,

A new, practical and original work on RURAL ARCHITECTURE, elegantly Illustrated with 150 *Designs and Plans of Houses of Moderate Cost*, including Stables and Out-Buildings, with a Chapter on the Construction of "Balloon Frames." PRICE $1.50 MAILED FREE TO ANY ADDRESS.

MANUAL OF THE HOUSE.

Or how to build Country Houses and Out-buildings, with 126 designs and plans, by D. H. Jacques. 12mo. 176 pages. Cloth, extra—post paid $1.50

GEO. E. & F. W. WOODWARD, Publishers,
37 Park Row, N. Y.

Advertising Sheet, Woodward's Annual.—1867.

ESTABLISHED IN 1846,

"The Horticulturist."

MONTHLY—TWO DOLLARS AND FIFTY CENTS PER ANNUM.

TWENTY-SECOND ANNUAL VOLUME—1867.

A permanent, reliable and first-class magazine, published monthly, at TWO DOLLARS AND FIFTY CENTS per Annum, and devoted to the ORCHARD, VINEYARD, GARDEN and NURSERY; to *Culture under Glass, Landscape Gardening, Rural Architecture, and the Embellishment and Improvement of Country, Suburban and City Homes.*

Handsomely Illustrated !

Every one who has an Acre Lot, a Garden, a Fruit Farm, a Vineyard, a House to Build, Out-Buildings to Erect, a Home to Embellish and Beautify, will need the HORTICULTURIST for 1867.

1867—Two Dollars & Fifty Cents ; 1866 bound and post-paid, and 1867—$4.50 ; 1865 and 1866 bound and post-paid, and 1867 - $6.

The three volumes contain 1,200 royal octavo pages of reading matter from the best writers in the country, handsomely illustrated, a valuable series for every library.

GEO. E. & F. W. WOODWARD, Publishers,
37 *PARK ROW*, *New York.*

Agricultural, Horticultural and Architectural
BOOKS,

For Sale at Publishers' Prices at the Office of the Horticulturist, or mailed, post paid.

Orders executed for Books, Papers and Periodicals on any subject.

Grape Culture.

Culture of the Grape, by W. C. Strong, *new*	$3 00
Chorlton on Grape Culture under Glass	75
Fuller's Grape Culturist	1 50
Grapes and Wine, by Geo. Husmann, *new*	1 50
Haraszthy Grape Culture, Wine and Wine Making	5 00
My Vineyard at Lake View	1 25

Fruit Culture.

Barry's Fruit Garden	1 75
Bridgeman's Fruit Cultivators' Manual	75
Cole's American Fruit Book	75
Downing's Fruits and Fruit Trees of America	3 00
Eastwood on Cranberry	75
Elliot's Western Fruit Grower's Guide	1 50
Field's Pear Culture	1 25
Fuller on Strawberry	20
Hovey's Fruits of America, colored plates, 2 vols	35 00
Pardee on Strawberry	75
Rivers' Miniature Fruit Garden	1 00

Flowers.

Breck's New Book of Flowers	1 75
Bridgeman's Florists' Guide	75
Buist's Flower Garden Directory	1 50
Book of Roses, F. Parkman	3 00
Ladies' Flower Garden Companion, edited by Downing	2 00
Parlor Gardener	1 00
Rand's Flowers for Parlor and Garden	3 00
Rand's Garden Flowers	3 00
Skeleton Leaves and Phantom Boquets	2 00
Wax Flowers, and how to make them	2 00

Trees, &c.

Browne's Trees of America	6 00
Warder's Hedges and Evergreen	1 50

Rural Architecture.

Allen's Rural Architecture	1 50
Cleveland's Villas and Cottages	4 00
Cummings' Designs for Street Fronts, Suburban Houses and Cottages, with full exterior and interior details, 382 designs and 714 illustrations	10 00
Downing's Cottage Architecture	3 00
Downing's Country Houses	8 00
Hatfield's American House Carpenter	3 50
Leuchar's How to Build and Ventilate Hot-houses	1 50
Manual of the House, 126 designs and Plans cloth	1 50
Silloway's Modern Carpentry	2 00
Sloan's Homestead Architecture, 200 Engravings	4 00
Sloan's Ornamental Houses, 26 Colored Engravings	3 00
Vaux's Villas and Cottages, nearly 400 Engravings	3 00
Woodward's Country Homes	1 50
Woodward's Graperies and Horticultural Buildings	1 50

Agricultural, Horticultural and Architectural Books.

Landscape Gardening.

Downing's Landscape Gardening	$6 50
Kern's Landscape Gardening	2 00
Kemp's " "	2 00
Rural Essays by Downing	3 00
Smith's Landscape Gardening	1 60

Gardening, Horticulture, Agriculture, &c.

Allen's American Farm Book	1 50
Allen's Domestic Animals	1 00
American Rose Culturist	30
American Bird Fancier	30
Art of Saw-Filing	75
Bement's Rabbit Fancier	30
Bement's American Poulterer's Companion	2 00
Boursingault's Rural Economy	1 60
Boston Machinist, (W. Fitzgerald)	75
Brandt's Age of Horses, (English or German)	50
Bridgeman's Kitchen Gardeners' Instructor	75
Bridgeman's Young Gardeners' Assistant	2 00
Brown's Field Book of Manures	1 50
Buist's Family Kitchen Gardener	1 00
Burr's Field and Garden Vegetables of America	5 00
Burr's Garden Vegetables	2 50
Canary Birds, Manual for Birdkeepers	50
Carpenters' and Joiners' Handbook	75
Cobbett's American Gardener	75
Cole's Veterinarian	75
Coleman's Agriculture	4 00
Darlington's American Weeds and Useful Plants	1 75
Dana's Muck Manual	1 50
Dana's Essays on Manures	30
Dadd's Anatomy and Physiology of the Horse ... Plain	3 50
Dadd's Horse Doctor	1 50
Dadd's Cattle Doctor	1 50
Davies Preparation and Mounting of Microscopic Objects	1 50
Farmers' Every Day Book, octavo, 650 pages	3 00
Flint on Grasses and Forage Plants	2 50
Flint on Milch Cows	2 50
Flora's Interpreter and Fortuna Flora, (Mrs. Hale)	1 50
French's Farm Drainage	1 50
Garlick's Treatise on Propagation of Fish	1 25
Gray's Manual of Botany	4 50
Guenon's Treatise on Milch Cows	75
Harris'—Insects injurious to Vegetation ...... Plain Plates	4 00
" " " " Colored "	5 00
Harris' Rural Annual for 1866	25
Herbert's Hints to Horsekeepers	1 75
Hooper's Dog and Gun	30
How to Get a Farm, and Where to Find it	1 75
How to Write, Talk, Behave and do Business	2 25
Ik Marvel's Farm of Edgewood	2 00
Insect Enemies of Fruit Trees, (Trimble)	8 00
Jennings on Cattle	2 00
Jennings on Swine and Poultry	2 00
Jennings on the Horse and his Diseases	2 00
Jennings' Horse Training Made Easy, new	1 25
Johnson's Elements of Agricultural Chemistry	1 25
Johnston's Agricultural Chemistry	1 75
Klippart's Farm Drainage	1 50
Klippart's Wheat Plant	1 50
Langstroth on the Honey Bee	2 00
Liebig's Natural Laws of Husbandry	1 50
Liebig's Familiar Letters on Chemistry	50

Agricultural, Horticultural and Architectural Books.

Linsley's Morgan Horses	$1 50
Manual of Agriculture, Emerson & Flint	1 50
" of Flax Culture	50
" of Hop Culture	40
" of the Farm.............cloth	1 00
" of the Garden "	1 00
" of Domestic Animals. "	1 00
Mayhew's Illustrated Horse Doctor	3 50
Mayhew's " Horse Management	3 50
Mayhew's Practical Book-Keeping for Farmers	90
Blanks for do do	1 20
McMahon's American Gardener	3 00
Miles on Horses Foot	30
Miss Hall, Cookery and Domestic Economy	1 50
Miss Beecher's Domestic Receipt Book	1 50
Miss Beecher's Domestic Economy	1 50
Morrell's American Shepherd	1 50
Munn's Practical Land Drainer	75
New Clock and Watch Maker's Manual	2 00
Norton's Scientific Agriculture	75
Onion Culture	25
Orchard House Culture, by C. M. Hovey	1 25
Our Farm of Four Acres, paper, 30 cents; bound	60
Our Farm of Two Acres	20
Quinby's Mystery of Bee-keeping	1 50
Quincy Soiling of Cattle	1 25
Portfolio Paper File, (*Country Gentleman*)........$1 and	1 50
Peddler's Land Measurer, for Farmers	60
Phenomena of Plant Life, (Geo. H. Grindon)	1 00
Randall's Fine Wool Sheep Husbandry	1 00
Randall's Sheep Husbandry	1 50
Ready Reckoner	50
Richardson, On Dogs	30
Rivers' Orchard House	50
Schenck's Gardeners' Text-Book	75
Shepherds' Own Book	2 25
Skilful Housewife	75
Stewart's Stable-Book	1 50
Saunders' Domestic Poultry.........paper 40c. cloth	75
Sparrowgrass Papers	2 00
Ten Acres Enough	1 50
Tenny's Natural History and Zoology	3 00
Thompson's Food of Animals	1 00
Tobacco Culture	25
Todd's Young Farmer's Manual	1 50
The Great West	1 00
Tucker's Annual Register of Rural Affairs, Nos. 1 to 12, each	30
Tucker's Rural Affairs, Four Bound Vols., each containing three numbers of the Annual Register, printed on larger and finer paper, per vol.	1 50
Turner's Cotton Planter's Manual	1 50
Waring's Elements of Agriculture	1 00
Watson's American Home Garden	2 00
Wet Days at Edgewood, by Ik Marvel	2 00
Wetherell on the Manufacture of Vinegar	1 50
Youatt on the Horse	1 50
Youatt on the Dog	2 00
Youatt and Martin, On Cattle	1 50
" " On the Hog	1 00
Youatt, On Sheep	1 00
Youmans' Household Science	2 25
Youmans' New Chemistry	2 00

Address,   **GEO. E. & F. W. WOODWARD,**
PUBLISHERS, 37 PARK ROW, NEW YORK.

www.ingramcontent.com/pod-product-compliance
Lightning Source LLC
Chambersburg PA
CBHW020107170426
43199CB00009B/425